D0859541

B R O O K L Y N

BROOKLYN

A Journey Through the City of Dreams

J U D I T H   S T O N E H I L L   *and*   F R A N C I S   M O R R O N E

U N I V E R S E

Page 1: James and John Bard. *Steamboat Brooklyn of the Fulton and South Ferry Company.* c. 1846–49. The Brooklyn Historical Society.

Page 2: Brooklyn Heights houses. c. 1930s. New York Bound Archives.

Page 3: Williamsburg Bridge vintage postcard. 1912. Private collection.

Right: David Levine. *Atlantis*. 1967. Brooklyn Museum of Art.

Following spread: Nicholas Evans-Cato. *Parking Lot*. 2001. George Billis Gallery, New York.

First published in the United States of America in 2004 by

UNIVERSE PUBLISHING
A Division of Rizzoli International Publications, Inc.
300 Park Avenue South • New York, NY 10010
www.rizzoliusa.com

Copyright © 2004 Judith Stonehill and Francis Morrone

2004 2005 2006 2007 2008/
10 9 8 7 6 5 4 3 2 1
ISBN: 0-7893-1068-6

Editor: Ellen Cohen
Designed by Paul Kepple @ Headcase Design
www.headcasedesign.com

Printed in Hong Kong

Brooklyn: A Journey Through the City of Dreams is part of a series of New York Bound books.

CONTENTS

Introduction:

CITY OF DREAMS

Brooklyn's unique history, first as a collection of towns and country villages dating back to the seventeenth century, then as one of the great American cities, and now as the most populous (2,465,326 inhabitants) and bold-spirited borough of New York City, yields a place of rich history, proud people, magnificent architecture, cultural treasures, and beguiling lore.

In this book, we highlight the infinitely rich culture of Brooklyn. In pictures and words, we take you on an unexpected journey through a place that is also a state of mind, where the whole American experience is compressed into 81 square miles of beauty, wonder, sorrow, surprise, despair, enchantment, ambition, and, above all, dreams.

LITERARY LANDSCAPE

So many novelists, playwrights, and poets have written about Brooklyn that this paradoxical place is familiar even to those who know it only from books.

Readers may know Hart Crane's Brooklyn Bridge, "across the harbor, silver-paced," visible from his window on Columbia Heights; the old sycamores and maples shading the sidewalks near Prospect Park, reminding William Styron of a southern city; the nighttime musings of Truman Capote, "when the wind brings

Brooklyn Bridge, New York.

the farewell callings of boats outward bound"; the boyhood summers of Alfred Kazin, as he "went up and down the sands of Coney Island selling Eskimo Pies, or stopped in the Brooklyn Museum to look at the Ryders."

Writers linked to Brooklyn are legion. Arthur Miller, Norman Mailer, Bernard Malamud, Thomas Wolfe, and Derek Walcott. Carson McCullers, who unforgettably wrote that contrasting Brooklyn to Manhattan is "like comparing a comfortable and complacent duenna to her more brilliant and neurotic sister." Henry Miller, Betty Smith, Isaac Bashevis Singer, Woody Allen, and Paula Fox. Pete Hamill, who defined the essential Brooklyn style as "an irresistible (for a writer) combination of toughness and lyricism." Luc Sante, Paul Auster, Siri Hustvedt, Charles Siebert, Thulani Davis, Phillip Lopate, Colson Whitehead, and Jonathan Lethem, not to mention all the young writers in Park Slope and Fort Greene waiting to be discovered.

(Above) Brooklyn Bridge vintage postcard. c. 1900. Private collection. (Opposite) Joseph Stella. *Luna Park*. c. 1913. Whitney Museum of American Art.

Beyond these, there are three writers who inextricably belong to Brooklyn: Walt Whitman, Marianne Moore, and Richard Wright.

🦃 🦃 🦃 🦃 🦃

Walt Whitman, one of America's greatest poets, moved to Brooklyn as a young boy. Born in 1819 on a farm near Hempstead, Long Island, Whitman was four years old when he and his family came to the booming settlement of Brooklyn, then a village of about 12,000 people. By 1861, when he left, Brooklyn was the nation's third-largest city, with a population of about 280,000.

His father's continuous failures in business required the family to move from one Brooklyn street to the next—Front, Cranberry, Johnson, Tillary. When he was eleven years old, Walt Whitman left school and became an apprentice printer, which propelled him into a life of newspaper writing and editing. Such work, in turn, fed his literary aspirations. During his early years, Whitman taught at country schools and then returned to news-

paper work, writing for a variety of journals. He bought a press and fonts to start his own newspaper in Huntington, Long Island, delivering his papers on horseback throughout the countryside. In 1846, he began a two-year stint as editor of the *Brooklyn Eagle*.

Eventually Whitman decided to put newspaper work aside. He did freelance writing, book reviews, political squibs, and operatic criticism to earn money, as he focused upon poetry, experimenting in a style that was part prose and part verse. Perhaps the most hallowed literary site in Brooklyn is the southwest corner of Fulton and Cranberry Streets, in Brooklyn Heights, the location of the print shop where Whitman himself set the type for the first edition of *Leaves of Grass* in 1855. (The building was demolished in 1964, replaced by an apartment complex called Whitman Close.)

Fewer than a thousand copies were printed. Some bookstores refused to sell the book because of its "irreligious" tone, while the reviewers outdid each other in heaping scorn upon what they called

(Above) *Walt Whitman.* **1855. From first edition of** *Leaves of Grass.* **Library of Congress.**

an affront to respectable people. Whitman himself wrote that *Leaves of Grass* "arose out of my life in Brooklyn and New York . . . with an intimacy, an eagerness, an abandon, probably never before equaled."

The book's frontispiece photogravure, showing the poet rakishly wearing a cocked hat and open shirt, scandalized the genteel literary establishment of New York nearly as much as did Whitman's "wild" vers libre. Ralph Waldo Emerson and a few New England writers championed Whitman. Reviewing *Leaves of Grass*, a Boston writer declared

"it is a mixture of Yankee transcendentalism and New York rowdyism and, what must be surprising to both these elements, they seem to fuse with the most perfect harmony."

Earning little from the publication of *Leaves of Grass*, Whitman returned to journalism. He became editor of the Brooklyn *Daily Times* in 1857 and wrote provocative editorials protesting social abuses and championing civic improvements in Brooklyn. He would later describe his life during this decade as "curiously identified with Fulton Ferry . . . almost daily, I cross'd on the boats, often up in the pilot houses." This river crossing, amid thronging commuters and swooping gulls, excited poetic rhapsodies rarely equaled in American literature.

Stand today on the reconstructed pier at the foot of Old Fulton Street and imagine the river in Whitman's day, "the hurrying, splashing sea-tides—the changing panorama of steamers, all sizes, often a string of big ones outward bound to distant ports—the myriad of white-sail'd schooners, sloops, skiffs, and the marvelously beautiful yachts—the majestic sound boats as rounded the Battery and came along toward 5, afternoon, eastward bound."

(Above) *View of the Fulton Ferry buildings, Brooklyn, Long Island*. 1857. The New York Public Library.

A legendary fan of the Brooklyn Dodgers, the poet Marianne Moore lived for over thirty-five years on a quiet street near Fort Greene Park. Born near St. Louis, Missouri, in 1887, Moore attended Bryn Mawr College before moving to Greenwich Village and becoming editor of the literary magazine *The Dial*. A friend described her at this time as "an astonishing person with Titian hair . . . and a mellifluous flow of polysyllables which held every man in awe." Moore moved to Brooklyn with her mother in 1929, to a spacious apartment at 260 Cumberland Street in the Fort Greene neighborhood.

Marianne Moore became that rarest of creatures: a modernist poet of both high seriousness and popular appeal. An exponent of clear imagery, precise observation, and plain syntax, Moore's poetry had a technical virtuosity appreciated by other poets, many of whom were her friends.

Not at all a bohemian, Marianne Moore nonetheless cut an idiosyncratic figure in her flowing cape and black velvet hat—particularly when she sat in the grandstand at Ebbets Field, cheering

on her beloved Dodgers. During the 1956 World Series, she exhorted the Dodgers to win in her poem "Hometown Piece for Messrs. Alston and Reese" (shortstop Pee Wee Reese was always her favorite player). Moore once explained her affinity for athletes in relation to her liking for animals: "They are subjects of art and exemplars of it . . . minding their own business." The animal kingdom appeared in many of her poems, just as dozens of small animals in glass, ivory, and ebony, together with a live alligator, inhabited her apartment.

By the 1950s, Moore was a public figure, receiving dozens of letters a day from aspiring writers and autograph seekers. She won the Pulitzer Prize, the National Book Award, and the Bollingen Prize for her poetry, as well as numerous honorary degrees. As a Brooklyn resident, she continued to involve herself in civic causes, particularly the beautification of the parks. She especially loved Prospect Park. When the Parks Department threatened to raze the park's beautiful boathouse, Moore spearheaded the movement to preserve the building. Today, the boathouse shines anew as an Audubon Society birding station. Moore is also credited for her work in saving Brooklyn's gnarliest tree, the fabled Camperdown elm in Prospect Park (she wrote about "the intricate pattern of its branches" in a poem about this tree).

Moore moved back to Greenwich Village toward the end of her life. Her funeral rites took place in 1972 at Brooklyn's Lafayette Avenue Presbyterian Church, where she had attended services every Sunday morning and Wednesday evening for decades. She is still remembered in Fort Greene today. On the outside of her home at 260 Cumberland Street, there is a plaque with her own words:

"Brooklyn has given me pleasure, has helped educate me; has afforded me, in fact, the kind of tame excitement on which I thrive."

🦉 🦉 🦉 🦉 🦉

Richard Wright wrote *Native Son*, the book that made him famous, in Fort Greene, Brooklyn. He moved to 175 Carleton Avenue in 1938, into a large room at the back of a brownstone house. He typically rose at dawn and walked to nearby Fort Greene Park with a lined yellow pad, a fountain pen, and a bottle of ink. Climbing to the top of the hill, he spent the morning writing—close to the Prison Ship Martyrs Monument that stands proud against the Brooklyn sky. Designed by Stanford White, the high column commemorates the 11,500 patriot soldiers who died in wretched conditions on British prison ships moored in nearby Wallabout Bay during the Revolutionary War.

Richard Wright had also experienced wretchedness. Born in 1908 to an illiterate Mississippi sharecropper, he had endured dire poverty, indifferent schooling, and violent racial discrimination. Joining the "Great Migration" from the South to Chicago, he worked at menial jobs when he published his first stories. When he came to New York in the late 1930s, Wright worked for the WPA Federal Writers Project and wrote the sec-

tion on Harlem in the *New York City Guide*. He was fortunate to receive a $2,500 Guggenheim grant, which supported him for a year and allowed him to finish *Native Son*.

Chosen as a Book-of-the-Month title, *Native Son* received extraordinary acclaim when it was published in the spring of 1940. It sold over 215,000 copies in its first three weeks. Reviewers described it as "powerful, disturbing, unquestionably authentic" and compared Wright to Dostoevsky. Wright later adapted the novel into a Broadway play, directed by Orson Welles, with great notices but a short run. When Hollywood became interested in making a movie of *Native Son*, MGM offered $25,000 if they could film it with an all-white cast. Wright refused.

Wright and his wife Ellen continued to live in Brooklyn during these years, at 11 Revere Place and then at 7 Middagh Street, the early nineteenth-century frame house celebrated for its

(Above) Gordon Parks. *Richard Wright*. 1943. Library of Congress.

bohemian occupants. (The house was torn down two years later, in 1945, for the Brooklyn–Queens Expressway). At one time or another Carson McCullers lived there, along with W. H. Auden, Paul and Jane Bowles, the theatrical designer Oliver Smith, and the house's owner, the literary editor George Davis, and his girlfriend, Gypsy Rose Lee. The Wrights lived there for only a year as they thought that it was "not a fit environment" for their young daughter. Richard Wright and his family then moved to an apartment building at 89 Lefferts Place in the Bedford-Stuyvesant section of Brooklyn, the same street where he'd lived five years before.

THE MARTYRS MONUMENT, BROOKLYN, N.Y.

After *Native Son*, Wright wrote the narrative for *12 Million Voices*, a photo documentary of the black urban experience in the North. (The FBI considered his text to be dangerously radical and began following him). He published his autobiography *Black Boy* in the spring of 1945, and although Mississippi banned it, the book quickly rose to the top of every New York newspaper's best-seller list. In a review, Ralph Ellison suggested that Wright's narrative was like the blues— "an autobiographical chronicle of personal catastrophe expressed lyrically."

Wright left Brooklyn in 1945 and spent a year in Greenwich Village. He lived the rest of his life in Paris, dying there in 1960 at the age of fifty-two. He is buried there in Père Lachaise Cemetery.

(Above) Fort Greene: The Martyrs Monument vintage postcard. Private collection.

GREEN SPACES

Nature takes over in the summertime when Brooklyn seems painted a hundred shades of green. Behind the rows of houses bloom lush gardens and shady trees. Oak and cherry trees line the sidewalks, a reminder of the forest that once grew here. To look down upon Brooklyn, with a bird's eye view, one would think the borough itself a park.

Brooklyn's famous backyard tree is the humble ailanthus, considered a weed by botanists but prized by urbanites for its ability to withstand just about anything. The ailanthus is a true city tree, and no account of Brooklyn's green spaces could fail to mention *A Tree Grows in Brooklyn*, Betty Smith's bittersweet novel of Irish immigrant life in turn-of-the-twentieth-century Williamsburg. "The one tree in Francie's yard was neither a pine nor a hemlock. It had pointed leaves which grew along green switches which radiated from the bough and made a tree which looked like a lot of opened green umbrellas. Some people called it the Tree of Heaven." The ailanthus gives delight and hope to the book's heroine, an eleven-year-old girl who likes to imagine—perched high on a tenement fire escape—that she is living in a tree.

PROSPECT PARK

As Brooklyn became a city and grew in the 1830s and '40s, there was much countryside throughout Kings County, most of which remained largely rural until the end of the nineteenth

century. But there was very little open space designed for recreation or contemplation.

Henry Evelyn Pierrepont, of the prominent landowning Brooklyn Heights family, served on the commission that mapped the new city's streets and squares. His visionary idea of building a great cemetery resulted in the creation of Green-Wood Cemetery in 1838. This in turn inspired the public-parks movement in this country, since the cemetery was immensely popular with the public as a place for promenading and picnicking. Set on a hilltop in the neighborhood we now call Sunset Park, Green-Wood's vast green expanses, beautiful monuments, and wooded bowers proved irresistible to those wishing a Sunday stroll, a lover's retreat, or a family outing.

Many Brooklynites—including Walt Whitman, as editor of the *Eagle*—began to campaign for a proper park. Their efforts

(Above) Prospect Park vintage postcards. Private collection.

resulted in the opening of Fort Greene Park (then called Washington Park) in 1850. Like Green-Wood Cemetery, it sits upon a hill, with magnificent views in all directions. Still, Fort Greene Park, popular as it was (and is), was but a small park. Manhattan, meanwhile, was building Central Park, a greensward of metropolitan scale.

The president of Brooklyn's park board, a civic leader named James S. T. Stranahan, invited architect Calvert Vaux—the designer of Central Park, along with Frederick Law Olmsted— to consult on a plan for creating Prospect Park. Vaux became involved in the land-acquisition process and in setting the park's boundaries. Remembering how

well his partnership had worked for the Manhattan project, he asked Olmsted to join him in Brooklyn. By then, Vaux had largely designed a park of 526 acres on the west side of Flatbush Avenue.

Some say that Prospect Park is the most perfect urban park in the United States. Vaux and Olmsted themselves held it to be far superior to Central Park. Like all of their creations, it is a romantic confection, based on eighteenth-century British landscape designs. The contours are irregular. Spaces merge into one another to surprise and beguile the visitor. Parks are viewed today as recreational places, for softball, frisbee, soccer, and cricket. (The last two, owing to Brooklyn's large West Indian population, are

(Above) Alexandra Stonehill. Photograph of the Tennis House, Prospect Park, 2003.

WALK UNDER BRIDGE, PROSPECT PARK, BROOKLYN, N. Y.

often played in Prospect Park.) But for Olmsted and Vaux, parks were places of repose and contemplation. Their parks provided the respite of nature in the midst of the often noisome, unsanitary, teeming metropolis. Ironically, these slices of nature were anything but natural, as the landscape architects artfully arranged trees and shrubs, bodies of water and formations of rock, to offer the range of nature's delights in a way nature itself could not do within such confines.

Prospect Park divides roughly in thirds, each part dominated by a single feature: meadow, water, and forest. The desire to present the panoply of naturalistic effects led Olmsted and Vaux to incorporate elements both pastoral and dramatic. Perhaps Prospect Park's most popular feature is its Long Meadow, bordering the Park Slope neighborhood. Here is a magnificent sweep of rolling greenery, funneled now and again through stands of trees. There is the sense of infinite expanse, of vistas awaiting discovery. In the central swath of the park we find water, lakes and ponds and burbling streams, water splashing rock. Here were the boats that painter William Merritt Chase loved to depict, and that we see in the movie *Sophie's Choice*. Finally, there are the park's densely forested paths, self-conscious recreations of an Adirondack wilderness. The Ravine, recently so beautifully restored by the Prospect Park Alliance, has the drama of a Thomas Cole painting.

Many people unthinkingly refer to "Olmsted's Prospect Park," not recognizing that the park owes its majesty to Vaux's artistry. Born in London in 1824, Calvert Vaux apprenticed to an architect when he was nineteen. He immigrated to America a few years later to become the assistant of Andrew Jackson Downing, the prominent landscape gardener—and within a few months was his partner. In 1858, when the city announced a public competition for the designing of Central Park, Vaux invited Olmsted to join him in preparing a plan. Their design, "Greensward," won. Seven years later, the two collaborated on Prospect Park. Later, Vaux and Olmsted planned Eastern Parkway and Ocean Parkway, great green boulevards conceived as part of a proposed metropolitan park system in which landscaped roadways would connect major parks throughout the city. They also worked together on two smaller park designs for Brooklyn, renovating Fort Greene Park and creating Tompkins Park in Bedford-Stuyvesant.

When the partnership ended, Vaux concentrated on designing buildings. He died in Brooklyn, in 1895, under mysterious circumstances. While visiting his son's home in the resort community of Bensonhurst-by-the-Sea, Vaux went out for a stroll on a

City Beautiful movement at the end of the nineteenth century had made his romantic English style of architecture unfashionable. He needn't have worried. Today, we prize Vaux's designs as works without which life in the city is unthinkable.

BROOKLYN
BOTANIC GARDEN

This may be the most peaceful

particularly foggy morning and apparently walked off the end of a pier into Gravesend Bay. When his body washed ashore days later, the authorities ruled the death an accident. Still, some speculated it was suicide. Vaux resented that Olmsted, a former journalist with a genius for publicity, always received credit for their joint designs. Also, he bridled at how the ascendance of the

place in Brooklyn, although 750,000 visitors come here annually to admire its 52 acres of idyllic gardens. Begun in 1910, the Brooklyn Botanic Garden is one of the premier botanical institutions in the world. Some visitors' favorite is the Bluebell Wood, planted under a stand of majestic oaks; many cherish the Cranford Rose Garden, containing over 5,000 specimens that bloom

(Above) William Merritt Chase. *Tompkins Park, Brooklyn*. c. 1886. Colby College Museum of Art.

through the summer; others prefer the famous collection of Japanese bonsai.

All of these are part of the thirteen "gardens within a garden," comprising 13,000 species of plants. Each garden is distinctive, ranging from the Herb Garden, an enclave with over 300 medicinal, culinary, and ornamental herbs, to the Shakespeare Garden, which concentrates on plants mentioned in Shakespeare's sonnets and plays.

The Cherry Esplanade, a grove of Japanese cherry trees that bloom spectacularly in April and May, is one of the most popular attractions (causing traffic jams in Brooklyn). Each spring the Sakura Matsuri festival celebrates the cherry blossoming with centuries-old Japanese traditions that include classical dance, origami, and flower arranging. The cherry trees have even inspired a link to the Dodgers: when the city demolished Ebbets Field, trucks brought the stadium's sod to the Brooklyn Botanic Garden as topsoil to nourish these trees (or so the story goes).

Of special note is the splendid Japanese Hill-and-Pond Garden, built in 1915 to the designs of the landscape architect Takeo Shiota. Recently restored, this authentic "stroll garden" was inspired by those of the Edo period. Shiota said he wished to create "a garden more beautiful than all others in the world." This may be the most beloved of all the gardens at the Brooklyn Botanic Garden, beguiling many artists and writers. In *A Walker in the City*, Alfred Kazin remembered his first trip there, as a young schoolboy from Brownsville. "After we went through the bamboo gate into the Japanese Garden, crossed over a curved wooden bridge past the stone figure of a heron dreaming in the water, I lay in the grass waiting to eat my lunch out of the shoe box and wondered why water lilies floated half-submerged in the pond and did not sink."

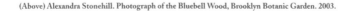

(Above) Alexandra Stonehill. Photograph of the Bluebell Wood, Brooklyn Botanic Garden. 2003.

GREEN-WOOD CEMETERY

Created as a place of "rural quiet, and beauty, and leafiness" in 1838, Green-Wood Cemetery retains its parklike beauty today. Its 478 acres of landscaped hills and winding paths, so enticing to naturalists and bird lovers, also attract urban historians and admirers of Victorian sculpture, drawn here by Green-Wood's extraordinary monuments. Grecian temples, obelisks, broken columns, cairns, and pyramids honor the 550,000 people buried here.

Famous people (Leonard Bernstein and Henry Ward Beecher). Infamous people (Boss Tweed and Joey Gallo). Fashionable people (Tiffanys and Havemeyers). Familiar names (F.A.O. Schwarz, Peter Cooper, Horace Greeley). Families (all four of the Brooks brothers). A large contingent from the Civil War (eighteen generals and a twelve-year-old drummer boy). Musicians, murder victims, and dozens of mayors. Ward McAllister, who defined society's Four Hundred. Henry Raymond, founder of *The New York Times*. The ragtime pianist Eubie Blake, who lived to be one hundred.

(Above) **Byron Studio**. *North Gate, Green-Wood Cemetery*. **1899. New York Bound Archives.**

Many artists are buried here: Jean Michel Basquiat, the young painter lionized during the 1980s art scene; William Merritt Chase, celebrated for his landscapes (including the parks of Brooklyn, in the late 1880s); John La Farge, renowned for his murals and stained-glass designs; Eastman Johnson, whose fashionable portraits commanded the highest prices of the nineteenth century; George Catlin, famous for his paintings of American Indians. Samuel F. B. Morse, an artist before he invented the telegraph. Asher Durand represents the Hudson River School, George Bellows the Ashcan School.

One of the most fascinating residents of Green-Wood may be Lola Montez (1824–1861), the legendary dancer and adventuress, notorious for her romantic liaisons with Franz Liszt, Alexandre Dumas, and Honoré de Balzac. She was also the mistress of King Ludwig of Bavaria, who gave her a palace and listened to her polit-

ical advice until a revolution ended his reign. And hers. Beautiful, head-strong, relentlessly ambitious, Lola performed her scandalous Spider Dance (which apparently involved much whirling of petticoats) on stages throughout Europe and America. The dance critics were unimpressed, but the audiences went wild. Lola spent her last years in New York, where she died penniless. Her modest marble gravestone is etched with only two words—her girlhood name, Eliza Gilbert.

Green-Wood Cemetery has three entrances, but the most impressive is the main entrance (Fifth Avenue and 25th Street) with its elaborate Gothic Revival gates, designed by Brooklyn architect Richard M. Upjohn in 1861. Perched in its spires are dozens of green parakeets that noisily welcome the funeral cortèges arriving here (over fifty funerals each week) and Green-Wood's many visitors.

(Above) *Lola Montez's Departure for America*. c. 1852. Private collection.

CONEY ISLAND

Coney Island is in the far south of Brooklyn, on the Atlantic Ocean. It isn't an island at all, but shares a peninsula with other fabled oceanfront communities, including Brighton Beach and Manhattan Beach.

The legendary period of Coney Island began in the late nineteenth century when, between 1897 and 1904, three spectacular amusement parks opened along Surf Avenue. Steeplechase, Luna Park, and Dreamland captured the imagination of millions and made Coney Island one of the most famous places on earth.

Steeplechase was the first great amusement park at Coney Island. Created by George C. Tilyou in 1897, the park was famous for its namesake ride, in which customers raced on wooden horses along high iron rails. Its attractions included a miniature steam railroad, an early roller coaster (the Scenic Railroad), and a salt-water swimming pool. Other crowd-pleasers were the Barrel of Love, the Earthquake Stairway, and the Human Roulette Wheel. In 1907, Steeplechase burned down. Rebuilt by Tilyou, the park opened in time for the 1908 summer season, bigger and better than ever. He added a more exciting steeplechase ride and the Pavilion of Fun, an indoor building that was the largest glass and steel structure of its time. Its nearly three acres of attractions included an Insanitarium, a Mechanical Jackass, and a Blowhole Theater.

The most popular of the amusement parks was Luna Park, which opened in 1903. By the next summer, it had an average daily attendance of ninety thousand. Frederick Thompson and Elmer "Skip" Dundy designed Luna Park as a fantasyland with all manner of exotic structures. "The architecture was a fantastic, almost nightmarish corruption of the Moorish and Byzantine in circus-clown colors of chalk white and cherry red with ornamental stripes of black and bright green on minarets, spires, and onion domes," wrote Joseph Heller in *Now and Then*, his memoir of Coney Island. Luna Park's attractions included an elaborate space-travel ride (A Trip to the Moon) and

the highest roller coaster in Coney Island (the Mile Sky Chaser). More than a million bare incandescent bulbs illuminated the park at night, outlining every structure with a dazzling display of light.

Dreamland had even more lights. The developer William H. Reynolds opened Dreamland in 1904, creating a neoclassical park that evoked the "City Beautiful" theme of Chicago's 1893 Columbian Exposition. Broad, uncongested avenues led crowds past the tall central tower (based on Seville's Giralda) to the mural paintings depicting the canals of Venice and the mountains of Switzerland. The classical theme extended to the amusements, including chariot races, although the Fighting Flames—with firemen rescuing women and children from a tenement in flames—was one of the most popular attractions. Steamboats brought crowds directly from the Battery, 23rd Street, and Harlem to Dreamland's two piers, but many visitors found this park less joyous than the other parks and it never turned a profit.

It seemed that everyone visited Coney Island during these golden years. P. G. Wodehouse enjoyed the "rollicking pleasure" of the Human Roulette Wheel; the Russian writer Maxim Gorky delighted

(Above) The Helter Skelter, Luna Park. 1905. New York Bound Archives.

(Above) Dreamland at Twilight. 1905. New York Bound Archives.

(Above) Coney Island vintage postcard. c. 1910. Rod Kennedy Collection. (Middle top) Night Scene in Dreamland vintage postcard. c. 1910. Private collection. (Middle bottom) Shoot the Chutes, Luna Park vintage postcard. 1912. Private collection. (Right) *The Colossal Elephant of Coney Island.* 1885. The New York Public Library. The elephant was built in 1885 as a small hotel, with a cigar store operating out of one front leg. The building burned down in 1894.

land, Coney Island, N.Y

COPYRIGHT 1908 ILLUSTR. POST CARD & NOV. CO. N.Y.

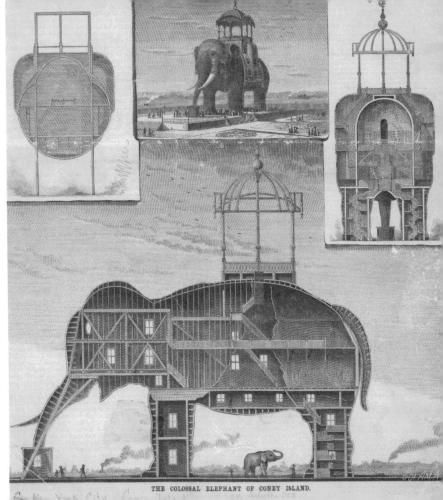

THE COLOSSAL ELEPHANT OF CONEY ISLAND.

in the sight of Luna Park at night, when "thousands of ruddy sparks glimmer in the darkness . . . ineffably beautiful"; and Sigmund Freud found Coney Island "ein grossartiger Wurstelprater" (a magnificent amusement park). "If Paris is France," boasted Steeplechase's George C. Tilyou, "then Coney Island, between June and September, is the world." Each summer, tens of thousands arrived daily

on the steamboats and streetcars to spend a few exhilarating hours in the three great amusement parks. Dreamland was the first to close, when it burnt down in 1911. Luna Park remained open until 1944, when fire destroyed most of the park. Steeplechase, "the Funny Place," closed last, in 1964.

Coney Island became known as the "Nickel Empire" in the 1920s, when rides at the amusement parks, hot dogs on the boardwalk, and the subway fare each cost five cents. After the BRT subway line reached Coney Island in 1920, the number of seaside visitors jumped from thousands of people to millions on a summer weekend, from then until the 1950s. "Come to Coney! The posters called, and everybody listened. And they came," wrote Norman Rosten in his novel *Under the Boardwalk*.

For many, Coney Island is synonymous with roller coasters, the most famous of which, the Cyclone, opened in 1927. One of

(Above) Milton Avery. *Steeplechase, Coney Island*. 1929. The Metropolitan Museum of Art.
(Opposite) Parachute Jump. 1955. Photograph from the *Brooklyn Daily Eagle*. Brooklyn Public Library, Brooklyn Collection.

the world's legendary roller coasters, it features 3,000 feet of track with nine drops. The top speed is 60 miles per hour, and the ride takes slightly less than two terrifying minutes. There have been over fifty roller coasters in Coney Island's history, but the Cyclone is by far the most ferocious coaster of all. As Charles Lindbergh said, "A ride on the Cyclone is greater than flying an airplane at top speed." During the 1960s, the city owned and operated the roller coaster, but closed it when its ridership declined and the structure deteriorated. When the city announced that it would demolish the Cyclone in 1972, Brooklynites staged a successful "Save the Cyclone" campaign and the coaster was privately leased. Restored and reopened in 1975, the Cyclone won official city landmark status in 1991.

Coney Island has two other cherished landmarks. The Wonder Wheel, a towering 150-foot-high Ferris wheel built by the Eccentric Ferris Wheel Company, opened in 1920. Its claim to fame went beyond its size, since the Wonder Wheel was innovative in the way the inner cars glide along a track as the wheel turns, adding a thrill to the ride. It has a perfect safety record. The only time it ever stopped was during the blackout on July 13, 1977, and the passengers got off when workers hand cranked the wheel. The Wonder Wheel was designated a city landmark in 1989.

The Parachute Jump, also designated as a city landmark in 1989, was one of the most famous attractions at Coney Island. Designed for the 1939 New York World's Fair in Flushing Meadow, the Parachute Jump was moved to Steeplechase Park in 1941.

Balmer's Bathing Pavilion. Coney Island, N.Y.

BALMER'S
GREAT ATLANTIC BATHING & SWIMMING BATHS

HOT & COLD SALT WATER BATHS.

Described as "the most exciting amusement ride of its generation," those daring to take the trip were pulled skyward to the top of the tower before plunging into a freefall, then finally hitting the ground with a jolt. The army used it in training paratroopers during World War II. The Parachute Jump remained a favorite Coney Island ride until 1964, when it closed. Nearly razed, it recently received a fresh coat of paint after two decades of neglect. Brooklynites think of its beautiful metal form, 262 feet in the air, graceful against the ocean sky, as their Eiffel Tower.

Coney Island's Boardwalk continues to delight today's generation of beachgoers. Opening in 1923, the Boardwalk extends 2.7 miles from Sea Gate to Brighton Beach. In its early days, summer visitors could be wheeled in a wicker chair along the walkway for 75 cents an hour. It is named after Edward J. Riegelmann, the Brooklyn borough president responsible for building it. The Boardwalk draws hundreds of thousands of spectators each year to its annual Mermaid Parade, which began in 1983. The boisterous parade takes place every June, on the first Saturday after the summer solstice.

One of the most popular things to do in Coney Island is to eat a hot dog. Nathan's Famous has stood on the corner of Surf and Stillwell since 1916, when Polish immigrant Nathan Handwerker opened his hot-dog stand. He had worked for Charles Feltman, considered the inventor of the hot-dog-on-a-bun and owner of a Coney Island restaurant. Handwerker marketed his hot dogs by hiring homeless men to dress as doctors and stand at the counter eating. He then announced that if doctors ate

(Above) Nathan's Hot Dog Stand, Coney Island. 1916. Collection of Nathan's Famous.

his hot dogs, they must be good for you. Nathan's inaugurated its annual Fourth of July hot-dog eating contest in 1916, the year the stand opened.

The New York Aquarium is a favorite attraction at Coney Island, with a famous collection of over 350 species of aquatic wildlife. This is the oldest continuously operating aquarium in the United States, first opening at Castle Clinton in Battery Park in 1896. It closed that site in 1941 during the construction of the Brooklyn–Battery Tunnel, moving temporarily to the Bronx Zoo. Finally, the aquarium opened in Brooklyn in 1957, on fourteen acres by the sea at West 8th Streeet and the Boardwalk. Now part of the Wildlife Conservation Society, the aquarium's extensive marine life collection includes penguins, seals, walruses, sea otters, giant turtles, 400-pound sandtiger sharks, Beluga whales (this was the first aquarium to breed and exhibit such whales), and a new exhibit on alien stingers. The Osborn Laboratories of Marine Sciences, part of the aquarium, currently studies coral reefs, dolphin cognition, and satellite tagging of sharks.

Coney Island's glory is not all in the past. Summer visitors today can ride the Cyclone, take a whirl on the Wonder Wheel, attend a ballgame at Keyspan Park, devour cotton candy and world-class pizza, gawk at the Mermaid Parade, go to one of the world's great aquariums, and walk along miles of sandy beach.

(Above) The Polar Bear Club, Coney Island. 1912. New York Bound Archives.

THE WATERFRONT

THE BROOKLYN NAVY YARD

Nothing on Brooklyn's waterfront quite compares to the New York Naval Shipyard, more familiarly known as the Brooklyn Navy Yard. The U.S. Navy ran the shipyard from 1801 to 1966. Its closing occasioned the same kind of gloom as the folding of the *Brooklyn Eagle*, the departure of the Dodgers, and the end of Steeplechase. How, without these icons, could Brooklyn continue to be Brooklyn?

The Navy Yard came to occupy 255 acres at Wallabout Bay, with Williamsburg to the north and Vinegar Hill to the south. Even in the yard's earliest days, the Navy maintained a fevered pace of production. Building more than a hundred ships for use in the war of 1812, the Navy went on to create its first ocean-going steamship, the Fulton, in 1814–15. The steamship *Niagara*, which helped to lay the Atlantic Cable, hailed from Brooklyn's Navy Yard.

During the Civil War, the Union Navy made Brooklyn its center of naval activity. In the peacetime 1880s, the Navy Yard became a tourist destination. Visitors could board the old frigate U.S.S. *Constitution* and promenade on the waterfront's manicured lawns. (William Merritt Chase created many paintings of proper Victorian ladies strolling about the Navy Yard.) A more martial time awaited, and in 1895 the navy launched the *Maine* from Brooklyn. The sinking

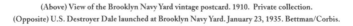

(Above) View of the Brooklyn Navy Yard vintage postcard. 1910. Private collection.
(Opposite) U.S. Destroyer Dale launched at Brooklyn Navy Yard. January 23, 1935. Bettman/Corbis.

DRY-DOCK AT THE NAVY YARD   BROOKLYN, N.Y.

mar. 12, 1906

a. R. Hand 4?H

GERMANY.
COPYRIGHT 1903 EUNIQUE MULLER.

of this battleship in Havana's harbor set off the Spanish-American War three years later.

Decades later, at the start of World War II, the Navy Yard greatly expanded its space by demolishing the Wallabout produce market. By 1944, more than 71,000 people worked in round-the-clock shifts at the Navy Yard. America's participation in World War II began and ended with ships from Brooklyn. The *Arizona*, destroyed at Pearl Harbor on December 7, 1941, came from Brooklyn. So did the *Missouri*, aboard which, on September 2, 1945, the Japanese signed the peace treaty ending the war.

The Navy Yard flourished during the 1950s, but by 1966 the Navy chose to move its activities to other ports. The Navy Yard, a fixture in Brooklyn for 165 years, closed.

Today, however, the Navy Yard thrives as a bustling industrial park, comprising nearly four million square feet in forty buildings. More than 3,000 people work here, producing prefab houses, artificial sweetener, museum-quality furniture, and television shows. Brooklyn knows how to adapt.

(Above) Dry Dock at the Brooklyn Navy Yard vintage postcard. 1903. Private collection.

WASHINGTON'S RETREAT FROM BROOKLYN

One of the boldest maneuvers of the Revolutionary War took place at the site of the Fulton Ferry Landing, when George Washington successfully led a retreat of the Continental army across the river after the Battle of Brooklyn. The victorious British wished to cut off the poorly equipped colonial forces from every escape route and would have captured them had they not fled from Brooklyn on the night of August 29, 1776.

Transporting 9,500 soldiers in secrecy across the East River—a mile wide, with strong currents, and controlled by a fleet of British warships—was a daunting challenge, particularly since the mission had to be completed in a single night. With only ten boats on hand, General Washington urgently requisitioned "every kind of water craft . . . that could be kept afloat and that had either sails or oars," to be brought to the east harbor of the city by dark.

That evening, at eight o'clock, the evacuation silently began— with orders conveyed in whispers, the oars of the rowboats muffled in cloth, and General Washington on horseback encouraging the regiments waiting to board. The armada of flatboats, schooners, sloops, and rowboats was buffeted by gale winds and strong currents until midnight, when calm waters and a southwest wind allowed the boats to go quickly back and forth—so heavily loaded with men and their equipment that "their gunwales were only three inches from the water."

At daybreak, thick fog miraculously hid the last boats to cross the East River. Of the nearly 10,000 soldiers that set out on the retreat from Brooklyn, the British wounded or captured only seven. A young American officer who fought in the Battle of Brooklyn later wrote, "In the history of warfare, I do not recollect a more fortunate retreat."

To appreciate General Washington's perilous retreat, one can go to the Fulton Ferry Landing (at the foot of Old Fulton Street) and stand on the pier. Sidewalk plaques describe the event.

BROOKLYN WHITE LEAD CO.

BROOKLYN WHITE LEAD Cos WORKS,
Front, Water, Adams & Washington Sts, Brookly

N.Y.

INDUSTRIES ON THE WATERFRONT

Brooklyn is not an island unto itself. Rather, it forms the western end of the four-county Long Island. Yet water surrounds Brooklyn on three sides. Ocean, harbor, river, canal, and creek are all utterly central to Brooklyn's identity, as water-bound as that of any city on earth.

Water-bound commerce was critical to Brooklyn's growth as a major industrial city. The port facilities, together with industries requiring a waterfront location, were crucial to this growth.

Greenpoint and neighboring Williamsburg, to the south, were home to the "black arts," industries that darkened the sky with soot and smoke. Chief among these was oil refining, with over fifty refiners operating along these shores. Most came under the ownership of the great oil monopolist, John D. Rockefeller. In 1879, Rockefeller ran an underground oil pipeline from the fields of Pennsylvania, across New Jersey, under the Hudson and East Rivers, to the Brooklyn shore. The most important of the Brooklyn refiners, Charles Pratt, founded the Astral Oil Works,

(Left) Brooklyn White Lead Co. Works trade card. c. 1890. Brian Merlis collection.

which produced the world's highest-quality kerosene. When Rockefeller's Standard Oil Company acquired Astral, Pratt became the richest man in Brooklyn. His philanthropy endowed Brooklyn with Pratt Institute, a renowned professional school of art, architecture, and engineering, located in the Clinton Hill neighborhood.

Another of the black arts was ironworking. Just north of the Pratt refinery stood the Continental Ironworks, where the Union Navy built the ironclad ship the *Monitor* during the Civil War. South of the Pratt refinery was the Hecla Architectural Iron Works, in operation from the 1870s to the 1920s. A thousand workers produced ornamental ironwork of the highest quality. All of the ornamental ironwork in Grand Central Terminal, for example, came from Williamsburg.

Porcelain and glass manufacturing were the other black arts. Thomas Smith, a Brooklyn architect, visited the great porcelain works at Sèvres and Staffordshire to learn all he could about the manufacture of fine porcelain. His Union Porcelain Works, in Greenpoint, became America's premier factory of hard porcelain. Collectors covet Union Porcelain pieces, now displayed in major museums. An exceptional example is the 1876 Century Vase, exhibited at the Brooklyn Museum of Art. Museums also display the wares created by Christian Dorflinger's Greenpoint Glass Works and of Brooklyn Flint Glass Works. (Flint later moved upstate and changed its name to Corning Glass.)

An important Williamsburg industry was (and is) sugar refining. A local street name— Havemeyer Street—refers to this

(Above) Devoe's Brilliant Oil Works, Brooklyn trade card. c. 1890. Brian Merlis collection.
(Opposite) Berenice Abbott. *Warehouse, Water and Dock Streets*. 1936. The Museum of the City of New York.

important industry. In the 1850s, Frederick Havemeyer opened a sugar refinery here that evolved into today's huge Domino Sugar Corporation. Some of the original buildings still stand among the more modern Domino structures, in the shadow of the Williamsburg Bridge.

Brewing was an industry with which we identify Brooklyn. It once boasted over forty-five breweries. German immigrants settled in Williamsburg and opened breweries, some of which—notably Schaefer and Rheingold—grew to be among the nation's largest. "Brewer's Row" emerged in Williamsburg. As American brewing became concentrated among a handful of vast commercial brewers, Brooklyn's brewing industry faltered, then disappeared. In the 1990s, a new golden age began, when microbreweries and craft breweries all over the country began to develop small-batch, high-quality beers and ales. Tom Potter and Steve Hinde's Brooklyn Brewery is one of these breweries, producing some of America's finest beers under brewmaster Garrett Oliver. The brewery is in a space once occupied by Hecla Iron Works.

The Brooklyn waterfront burgeoned with hundreds of factories and thousands of workers. The largest rope factory in the nation, the American Manufacturing Co., was located in Greenpoint near the world's largest manufacturer of pencils, Eberhard Faber, which flourished in Brooklyn for eighty-four years. The two most famous pharmaceutical companies in America had plants in Brooklyn: Pfizer in Williamsburg and Squibb in DUMBO. The country's largest producer of cardboard boxes, Gair Manufacturing, was also in DUMBO, near one of the biggest producers of tin cans, the E. W. Bliss factory.

The industrial waterfront of Red Hook was once a major port, with its Erie Basin and Atlantic Basin built to handle oceangoing vessels. The neighborhood teemed with workers and residents and a 24-hour-a-day dockside hum. This was the setting of Elia Kazan's film *On the Waterfront*, Arthur Miller's play *A View from the Bridge*, Hart Crane's poem "O Gowanus," and Hubert Selby Jr.'s novel *Last Exit from Brooklyn*. After World War II, shipping declined in Brooklyn. Its multistory warehouses couldn't accommodate the new container ships and this once bustling waterfront became derelict. The one exception is Brooklyn's lone container-port, a 100-acre facility in Red Hook that is now an international transshipping center for cocoa.

Sunset Park, between Red Hook and Bay Ridge, boasts two of the most impressive port facilities ever built. The

Bush Terminal complex comprised eighteen piers serving twenty-five steamship lines. Occupying over 200 acres, the terminal included warehouses, railroads, and its own steam and electrical plants. Today, like the Navy Yard, Bush Terminal is a thriving industrial park. Nearby are the buildings of the former Brooklyn Army Terminal, now an industrial and office complex, but once one of the U.S. Army's most important supply depots. From World War I to the Vietnam War, millions of army troops passed through the terminal. In 1958, the young draftee Elvis Presley met the press and some ardent fans in the Army Terminal before he boarded a troopship bound for Europe.

As the waterfront industries disappeared, mile after mile of waterfront became available for new uses. Artists and entrepreneurs are now adaptively reusing the old factory and warehouse buildings. Plans are afoot for a cross-harbor rail tunnel that may revive shipping and industry along some of the Brooklyn waterfront. The shoreline is Brooklyn's most precious resource, and the key to the borough's future, as to its past.

(Above) W.H. Bartlett and G.K. Richardson. *The Ferry at Brooklyn, New York*. 1838. Private Collection.

NEW YORK TOWER.

BROOKLYN TOWER.

AJOR, Publisher, 320 Pearl St., N.Y.

JOHN A. ROEBLING, C. E.   DESIGNER OF BRIDGE.
WASHINGTON A. ROEBLING,   CHIEF ENGINEER.
CHARLES C. MARTIN,   1ST ASST. ENGINEER.
FRANCIS COLLINGWOOD,   } ENGINEERS.
COL. WM. H. PAINE,   }
GEO. W. McNULTY,   }

WILLIAM VANDERBOSCH,   } DRAUGHTSMEN
WILLIAM HILDENBRAND,   }
E. F. FARRINGTON,   MASTER MECHAN.
THOS. G. DOUGLAS,   SUPT. OF MASON.
CHAS. W. YOUNG.   GENL. FOREMAN.

BIRD'S-EYE VIEW OF THE GREAT NEW YORK AND BROOKLYN BRIDGE,
AND GRAND DISPLAY OF FIRE WORKS ON OPENING NIGHT.

[PYROTECHNICS FURNISHED BY DETWILLER & STREET, NEW YORK.]

COMMENCED JANUARY 3, 1870.   FINISHED MAY 24, 1883.

The Bridge crosses the river by a single span of 1595 ft., suspended by four cables 15¾ in. in diameter; each cable consists of 5,434 parallel steel wires; ultimate strength of each cable 11,200 tons.   The approach on the New York side is 2,492½ ft., approach on the Brooklyn side 1,901 ft.,
total length 5,989 ft.   Size of towers at high water line 140x59 ft., total height of Towers 277 ft.   From high water to roadway 120 ft.,—from high water to centre of span 135 ft.,—from roadway to top 158 ft.,—width of Bridge 85 ft.,
with tracks for steam cars, roadway for carriages, and walks for foot passengers, and an elevated promenade commanding a view of extraordinary beauty and extent.   Cost, $15,000,000.

BRIDGES:

Colossal Feats of Engineering

The sight of Manhattan's amazing skyline of tall buildings thrills everyone who flies into New York at night. One's attention soon shifts, however, to an even more splendid sight: the bridges slung majestically across the rivers. Lit up at night, the bridges loop gracefully over the black background of water, producing a visual sensation unlike any other in the world. Most of these great bridges connect Brooklyn to other parts of the city.

Four suspension bridges in particular command our attention. First and foremost, of course, is the Brooklyn Bridge. To tell its story requires a book hundreds of pages long. (That book exists: *The Great Bridge* by David McCullough.) The "Great East River Bridge," as people called it in the beginning,

took shape between 1870 and 1883. With a main span of 1,595 feet, it was by far the longest suspension bridge ever built. People considered it one of the wonders of the world. Not only an engineering marvel, the bridge is also wondrously beautiful. The German engineer John Roebling, followed by his son, Washington Roebling, designed the bridge with great Gothic-pointed arches of stone, suspended between which is a spider's-weblike system of steel-wire cables, an endless fascination to artists and poets.

John Roebling died in a freak ferryboat accident just before work on the bridge got under way. His son, Washington, took over, but he too suffered injuries, contracting nitrogen narcosis

(Above) Brooklyn Bridge walkway. c. 1900. New York Bound Archives.
(Opposite) *Fireworks at the opening of Brooklyn Bridge, May 24th, 1883*. Museum of the City of New York.

("the bends") from his work in the caissons of the bridge's towers. Confined to his home on Columbia Heights, Washington sat at his window surveying the construction. When he needed to be on the site, his wife, Emily Warren Roebling (sister of a famous Gettysburg general commemorated in a statue in Grand Army Plaza), acted as his surrogate. Indeed, she became much more than that. She became a self-taught engineer and served a crucial role in seeing the bridge to completion.

The Williamsburg Bridge was the next of the great bridges, completed in 1903, with a central span (1,600 feet) just barely eclipsing that of the Brooklyn Bridge. Leffert L. Buck designed the Williamsburg, connecting Manhattan's Lower East Side with Brooklyn's Broadway. In the bridge's wake, Williamsburg effectively became an extension of the Lower East Side, with Jewish, Italian, and Irish immigrants crowding into the Brooklyn neighborhood.

Next, in 1909, came the Manhattan Bridge. It is beautiful in a different way from the Brooklyn Bridge. Rather than the earlier bridge's rugged simplicity, the Manhattan exhibits the Beaux-Arts style of Carrère & Hastings, who designed the bridge with the Latvian engineer Leon Moisseiff. At 1,470 feet, it is not as long as the other East River spans.

All three bridges boast pedestrian walkways affording some of New York's most spellbinding strolls. (The Manhattan's footpath closed in the 1960s, but reopened in 2001, just in time to serve as a major escape route on September 11 for lower Manhattan workers.)

Connecting Brooklyn to Staten Island is the Verrazano–Narrows Bridge. Looming majestically over the Bay Ridge neighborhood, the Verrazano dwarfs Brooklyn's other bridges. Indeed, it once dwarfed every other bridge in the world. With a central span of 4,260 feet, the Verrazano ranked as the world's longest suspension bridge from its 1964 opening until 1981. Its cables employ enough wire to wrap around the earth five times at the equator, or to stretch halfway to the moon.

Colossal feats of engineering, Brooklyn's bridges loop the earth and stir the soul.

Approach, Williamsburg Bridge, Brooklyn, N. Y.

Sea words, coast words, sloop words,
sailor's and boatman's words,
words of ships, are numerous in America.
One fourth of the people of these states
are aquatic—love the water,
love to be near it, smell it, sail on it,
swim in it, fish, clam, trade to and fro
upon it. To be much on the water,
or in the constant sight of it,
affects words, the voice, the passions.

— WALT WHITMAN

VIRTUE & VICE

"City of Homes and Churches"

In the nineteenth century and well into the twentieth, many Brooklynites proudly considered themselves a pious lot, especially compared to those who lived in the Gomorrah across the river. It is not surprising, therefore, that many of the most prominent Brooklynites, those with nationwide celebrity, were preachers.

Some were men very famous in their day, though largely forgotten now. An example is Richard Salter Storrs (1821–1900), for fifty-three years the pastor of Church of the Pilgrims in Brooklyn Heights (the church still stands today, on Clinton and Henry Streets). Storrs's fame came from his books and his preaching. Described by a contemporary as "combining a colossal intellect with a most benignant grace," he was among the multitude of New Englanders to leave his mark on nineteenth-century Brooklyn.

Over in Fort Greene, Theodore Ledyard Cuyler (1822–1909) led the flock at the Lafayette Avenue Presbyterian Church (still standing, on Lafayette Avenue and South Oxford Street). An abolitionist, he flew the Union flag over his church during the war. Brooklyn remembers him today in the name of Cuyler Gore, the small park at Fulton Street and Carlton Avenue.

At Central Congregational Church, Samuel Parkes Cadman (1874–1936) held the pulpit for thirty-six years. Cadman, a liberal activist and leader of the ecumenical movement, earned fame as America's first radio preacher. An audience of more than five million listeners tuned in every Sunday afternoon to hear this preacher with the famous rapid-fire delivery. Today's Cadman Plaza bears his name.

All of these clergymen pale in comparison, however, to Henry Ward Beecher, arguably the most famous American preacher of the nineteenth century—perhaps of all time. Beecher was born in 1813 in Litchfield, Connecticut, the son of a well-known preacher.

(Opposite) William Merritt Chase. *The Church of the Puritans.* 1887. Collection of George H. Meyer.

After graduating from Amherst, he followed his father's example by becoming a minister, starting out in Indianapolis. He earned a reputation as a revival preacher—a "circuit rider."

In 1847, he was called to Brooklyn to head the new Plymouth Church (still there today, on Orange Street). This austere Italianate structure, with its innovative, semicircular seating plan (designed to hold 2,800 people), suited his theatrical preaching style. Through his sermons at Plymouth Church and his weekly column in the Congregationalist publication *The Independent*, Beecher promoted his vision of a religion that appealed to the heart rather than the mind. His spellbinding oratory dazzled even Mark Twain, who described Beecher preaching to his congregation, "marching up and down the stage, sawing his arms in the air, hurling sarcasms this way and that, discharging rockets of poetry, and exploding mines of eloquence."

In the 1850s, Beecher became one of the nation's most influential opponents of slavery. He helped promote the antislavery novel *Uncle Tom's Cabin*, written by his sister Harriet Beecher Stowe, and worked in forming the new Republican Party. The public so closely identified him with the abolitionist movement that the guns shipped to Kansas by abolitionists for the use of antislavery activists became known as "Beecher's Bibles."

By war's end, Beecher was the most famous clergyman in America, identified with the progressive causes of abolition, women's rights, temperance, and expansion of educational opportunities. He was so popular that people called the Fulton Ferry "Beecher boats," as hordes descended upon Brooklyn on Sunday mornings to attend Plymouth Church, a short walk from the ferry landing on Fulton Street. Beecher's sermons were as great a tourist attraction as New York possessed in those days.

Not everyone loved Beecher. One such was the fiery feminist, spiritualist, Wall Street broker, confidante of Commodore Vanderbilt, and "free love" advocate Victoria C. Woodhull. The "free love" part, above all, caused Beecher to attack Woodhull in the pages of *The Independent* and allied publications. In 1872, Woodhull fired back. "My judges," she wrote, "preach against

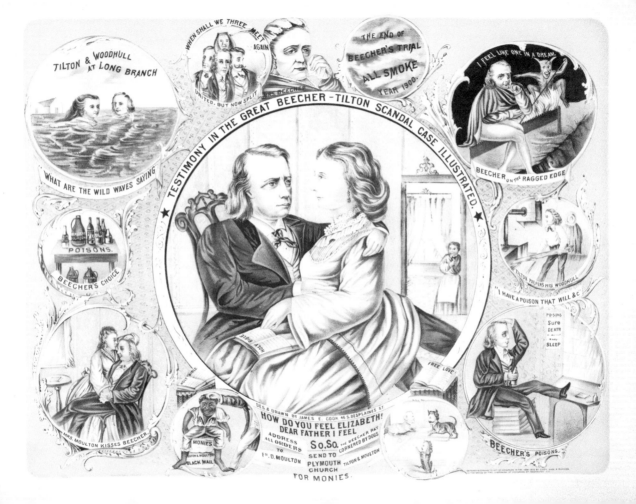

free love openly, and practice it secretly." She published her claim that Beecher was involved in an adulterous relationship with Elizabeth Tilton, the wife of Theodore Tilton, a prominent liberal editor and poet, who promptly sued Beecher for $100,000 in damages. A sensational court trial ended with Beecher's acquittal, although many would always presume that he was guilty as charged.

The trial nearly destroyed Beecher's public influence, although he worked hard to rebuild his reputation. During the 1870s and 1880s he styled himself a "Christian evolutionist," arguing that no fundamental conflict existed between Christian teachings and Darwin's recently expounded theories of evolution. When he died, in 1887, he was again the first citizen of Brooklyn. *Harper's Weekly* eulogized Beecher as a man "of strong virility, of exuberant vitality, of quick sympathy, of an abounding humor, of a rapid play of poetic imagination, of great fluency of speech."

A statue of Beecher—designed by the renowned sculptor (and onetime Brooklyn resident) John Quincy Adams Ward—stands

(Above) Beecher Statue in Downtown Brooklyn. c. 1910. New York Bound Archives.

today in Cadman Plaza. Henry Ward Beecher is buried in Brooklyn's Green-Wood Cemetery.

BROOKLYN GANGSTERS

Al Capone earned his greatest notoriety in Chicago, but he earned his stripes in his native Brooklyn. Of those stripes, none featured more in the Capone legend than the facial wound that earned him his famous moniker "Scarface."

The son of Neapolitan immigrants, Capone was born in 1899 in Vinegar Hill, at 95 Navy Street. Right in the heart of Brooklyn's "Barbary Coast," this commercial district featured tattoo parlors, dive bars, and brothels catering to sailors and waterfront workers. The Capone family moved to Brooklyn's Park Avenue and then to Garfield Place, near the Gowanus Canal. Young Alphonse went to school at P.S. 7 on Jay Street, but at age fourteen he got into a fight with a teacher and left school for good.

Capone joined a street gang called the South Brooklyn Rippers, who engaged in petty thievery, but he also worked at various jobs in the neighborhood (as a clerk in a candy store, a cutter in a bookbindery). Gangster Frankie Yale hired Capone to work as a bartender and bouncer at the Harvard Inn, a bar in Coney Island. In the summer of 1917, about a year after he started working there, Capone made a lascivious comment to a pretty girl seated at a table with her brother, a gangster named Frank Gallucio. The brother punched Capone, a fight ensued, and Gallucio slashed Capone's face three times with a knife. The legend of "Scarface" began in this Coney Island bar.

The mob bosses admonished Capone for his recklessness, but they recognized his potential as a strongarm. In 1920 Capone moved to Chicago, where his Brooklyn pal John Torrio was working in the underworld. "Terrible John" pioneered the corporate structure of organized crime. He was a "gentleman gangster," eager to keep his nefarious activities from public view as he maintained an outwardly respectable life as a family man and responsible citizen. Hired by Torrio to serve as his bodyguard and head his execution squad, Al Capone went on to become his partner. Eventually Torrio retired to Brooklyn, died a peaceful death, and was buried in Green-Wood Cemetery. Al Capone became the crime king of Chicago.

Brooklyn's most famous organized-crime figures were the infamous hired killers, active in the 1930s, dubbed by the *New York World–Telegram* as "Murder Incorporated."

Umberto and Anthony Anastasia were teenagers from Calabria when they stowed away on a cargo ship, alighting on the Brooklyn shore. Soon, the brothers ran rackets on the Brooklyn docks. The hardworking Umberto, who changed his name to Albert, caught the eye of Joe Masseria, one of New York's powerful crime bosses.

Another crime boss, Salvatore Lucanio, known as Lucky Luciano, wanted Masseria's empire. To get it, he invited Albert Anastasia to help him kill

(Right) Notorious Navy Yard Gang after confessing to murder of Brooklyn druggist. February 27, 1922. Bettmann/Corbis.

Masseria. In the shoot-out at Scarpato's, a restaurant on West 15th Street in Coney Island, Anastasia delivered the final blow, a shot to the back of the head. Luciano, wanting to protect his newly gained realm, then formed a group of contract killers to deal exclusively in murdering members of the mob. Murder, Inc. was created, with Albert Anastasia in control.

After the government deported Luciano back to Italy, Anastasia took control of his own "family." His underboss was a Brooklynite named Carlo Gambino. (More recently, John Gotti ran "the Gambino family.") In the course of a gangland power struggle, rival mobsters shot Anastasia as he sat in a barber's chair in a Manhattan hotel, with a hot towel draped on his face. The police never made an arrest in his murder. In 1957, Albert Anastasia was buried in Green-Wood Cemetery in a confidential location, as was traditional for underworld figures. (He is now listed on the official cemetery map.)

Based in Brownsville—working out of Midnight Rose's, an all-night candy store at the corner of Livonia and Saratoga Avenues—Murder Inc. earned a bloodcurdling reputation that came from their careful work. They flawlessly covered their tracks as they meted out mob justice to their employers' rivals and to informants. Fearing wiretaps, they invented an argot that we all know (a hit, for example, became a "contract"). They conformed to accepted gangland lore in their stout refusal to kill politicians, policemen, judges, and district attorneys, for fear of reprisals.

The group's most notorious member was a onetime soda-jerk

named Abe Reles, known as "Kid Twist." Strong and stocky, his large hands suited him well for strangulation, one of his specialties. Reles was also known for his precise use of an ice pick, inserted through a victim's ear to pierce his brain, and for burying a rival alive on a beach in Canarsie. In 1940, an informant led Kings County D.A. William O'Dwyer to arrest Reles. Turning on Murder, Inc. was Reles's only way to save his own life. The day before he was to testify in O'Dwyer's "airtight" case against Anastasia, in November 1941, under police protection, Abe Reles mysteriously fell six stories from Room 623 of the Half Moon Hotel at Coney Island. Mobsters called him "the canary that sang, but couldn't fly."

(Above) Gangsters linked to Brooklyn. May 2, 1933. Corbis.

BROOKLYN'S MASTER SPY

Colonel Rudolf Ivanovich Abel of the KGB, the highest-ranking Soviet spy ever captured in the United States, conducted his espionage from a small studio in Brooklyn for three and a half years. In 1953, using the alias Emil Goldfus, Abel rented space on the fifth floor of Ovington Studios at 252 Fulton Street for $35 a month.

Working in a building that was full of artists (including David Levine and Jules Feiffer), Abel was also known as an artist—indeed, he spent most of his time there painting. He became friendly with some of the young artists who worked in

the building, lending them paintbrushes and inviting them to his studio for coffee. They found him "a likeable guy," intelligent, modest, interested in talking about art—and seemingly apolitical.

Abel's arrest as a Soviet spy in 1957 astonished his artist-friends,

who had no idea that he stayed late in the studio several nights each week to receive short-wave radio messages from Moscow. When the F.B.I. searched his studio, they found a transmitter, coded messages, microfilm equipment, and maps of U.S. defense areas, as well as dozens of artists' paintbrushes and over fifty of his canvases (described by his fellow artists in the building as paintings with "a poor color sense" but much intensity).

During the court trial, authorities accused Abel of leaving coded messages at a drop point in Prospect Park, as well as many places beyond Brooklyn. Sentenced to thirty years in prison, Abel served five years before various agents arranged his exchange for Gary Powers, the American pilot whose U-2 reconnaissance plane was shot down over Russia. Abel returned to the Soviet Union in 1962.

(Above) Alexandra Stonehill. Montauk Club *(detail)*, Park Slope. 2003.

BROOKLYN DODGERS

Of America's great cities for baseball, Brooklyn is near the top of the list. What heartache for old Brooklynites that their city is without a major-league team today. How heartening, at the same time, that professional baseball has returned to Brooklyn, in the form of a minor-league team that has brought back the joys of the summer game.

Brooklyn had a leading role in baseball from the invention of the game, fielding its first team as early as 1849. Teams like the Eckfords (founded 1855), the Atlantics (an 1860s powerhouse), the obscure Gladiators, the Wonders, the Tip-Tops, and the Dodgers forerunners called the Bridegrooms and Superbas all called Brooklyn their hometown and were among the early professional franchises. Brooklyn's first baseball superstar was native son Wee Willie Keeler (so-called because he was only 5 feet 4 inches tall), compiler of the fifth best lifetime batting average in baseball history (.345), who famously said "I hit 'em where they ain't." Keeler starred in the 1890s, well before Ebbets Field rose near Prospect Park.

The Dodgers (so named in 1911) hung around—for a while at least. Today they are the Dodgers of Los Angeles. Yet the very name was Brooklyn-specific, short for "trolley dodgers," from the days when trolley tracks crisscrossed the borough—and took people to games at Ebbets Field.

(Above) Brooklyn baseball team. 1899. New York Bound Archives. (Opposite) Ebbets Field, Brooklyn vintage postcard. 1943. Private collection.

Ebbets Field was one of the first great modern ballparks. When such parks were new, they were utterly unlike any structures their cities had ever seen. The parks were huge in their neighborhood settings, with outer walls often detailed in classical styles. Ebbets Field, with its stately arcades, evoked Verona's Palazzo Consiglio of the fifteenth century. Inside, steep views down onto verdant playing fields, surrounded by ranks of wind-blown flags and immense scoreboards, provided perspectives that in themselves were worth the price of admission. When the delicate balletic geometries of America's sport took place upon the green background, it seemed that one witnessed not merely the exertions of gifted athletes, but something like art.

Charles Hercules Ebbets, a bartender's son from Greenwich Village, started out as a team employee selling peanuts at games. He rose in the ranks, and when the principal owner died in 1897, Ebbets owned ten percent of the stock and became club president. By 1900, Ebbets was the principal owner. He broke ground for the new ballpark, on a site bounded by Bedford Avenue, Sullivan Place, McKeever Place, and Montgomery Street in 1912. The next year, he dedicated the stadium—which eventually accommodated 31,497 spectators—as the Dodgers took to the field against the Philadelphia Phillies. Ebbets became a prominent Brooklynite, serving as a state assemblyman and city councilman. On the day of his funeral, in 1925, the National League cancelled all its games—something that is inconceivable today.

The next great leader of the Dodgers was Leland Stanford MacPhail, a lawyer and World War I officer. He took over as general manager in 1938 and introduced night baseball to Brooklyn that same year. Slowly, he led a struggling franchise on an upward course. He named shortstop Leo Durocher as manager. Known as "Leo the Lip," this colorful, irascible manager, who hung out with Humphrey Bogart and liked to fight with umpires, led the Dodgers into their golden age. With first baseman Dolph Camilli and outfielder Pete Reiser, Durocher's Dodgers won the National League pennant in 1941.

In the 1930s, New York's three teams (Dodgers, Yankees, and Giants) agreed not to allow radio to broadcast their games, fearing

(Opposite) Leo Durocher at a Brooklyn Dodgers baseball game. 1942. Hulton-Deutsch Collection/Corbis.

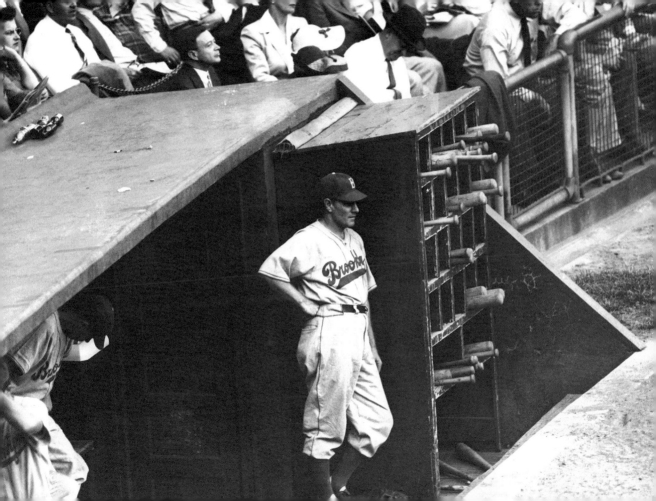

a decline in attendance. But in 1939, MacPhail hired the legendary Red Barber to broadcast Dodgers' games on the radio. When MacPhail left the Dodgers for the Yankees, his departure created an opening for Branch Rickey, the greatest of all Dodger leaders.

Rickey was an innovator, the first to broadcast baseball games on radio (in 1927). He also invented the minor-league, or "farm," system of modern baseball. In 1942, Rickey became president and general manager of the Brooklyn Dodgers. (He later was a co-owner.) He shocked the world by signing an African-American, Jackie Robinson, to a contract with the Dodgers' minor-league team, the Montreal Royals, in 1945; two years later, Robinson joined the Dodgers, and baseball's color barrier disappeared. In 1947, the Dodgers enjoyed their greatest attendance ever, as the exciting Robinson embarked on his Hall-of-Fame career, and the Dodgers continued their ascent as one of baseball's most victorious teams. It wasn't easy. Many fans and fellow players resented Robinson for his color and subjected him to verbal taunts and even physical abuse. Ever dignified, and a great baseball player, Robinson withstood the taunts and abuse, and soon many other black players joined him in the big leagues. In 1948, the great African-American catcher Roy Campanella became a Dodger, while pitcher Don Newcombe arrived the following year.

The 1950s were the Dodgers' glory years, as they achieved a level of year-to-year greatness with a cast of lovable players indelibly imprinted on the minds of old Brooklynites. The small outfield dimensions of Ebbets Field, dictated in part by the stadium's location in a densely developed neighborhood, made the stadium a hitters' paradise. The Dodgers won the pennant in Jackie Robinson's rookie year (although they lost the World Series to the arch-rival Yankees). From then until 1957, the Dodgers did not post a losing record, winning six pen-

(Opposite) William Klein. Dodgers fans at Ebbets Field, 1955. Courtesy Howard Greenberg Gallery, New York.
(Above) Jackie Robinson after scoring a home run. August 4, 1948. New York Bound Archives.

nants and one World Series (1955) in eleven years. Players included first baseman Gil Hodges (for whom a bridge in Brooklyn is named), shortstop Pee Wee Reese, slugging outfielder Duke Snider (a.k.a. the "Duke of Flatbush"), outfielder Carl Furillo (who batted .344 in 1953), and pitchers Preacher Roe (who in 1951 posted a 22–3 record), Ralph Branca (who allowed the infamous home run to the Giants' Bobby Thomson), Carl Erskine, Clem Labine, Johnny Podres, Sal Maglie (known as "Sal the Barber"), and Don Drysdale. None of these great players, however, was a Brooklyn native. The hometown crowd pinned their hopes on a wildly talented, handsome Jewish boy from Bensonhurst named Sanford ("Sandy") Koufax, who made a name for himself at the Parade Grounds at Prospect Park. Fulfilling his childhood fantasy, Sandy Koufax debuted with the Dodgers in 1955 and pitched at Ebbets Field for three years.

On September 24, 1957, the Dodgers played their last game at Ebbets Field. On that night, the Dodgers' Danny McDevitt hurled a five-hit shutout against the Pittsburgh Pirates. A paltry 6,702 spectators sat in the stands. Organist Gladys Gooding, who had whipped up the Dodger fans for nineteen years with her rousing organ-music, played tunes with a farewell theme: "Am I Blue?," "Don't Ask Me Why I'm Leaving," "Thanks for the Memories," and, most poignantly, "When I Grow Too Old to Dream." At game's end, Gladys concluded with "Auld Lang Syne." The Brooklyn Dodgers were history.

The next day, Carl Furillo said, "This is a sorry bunch to have to leave here. It is a good town."

In Jackie Robinson's rookie year, 1947, the number of spectators viewing the Dodgers at Ebbets Field totaled 1,807,526. In 1957, their last year in Brooklyn, the Dodgers drew only 56 percent of that number. It was a number no business could justify—especially as Dodgers' management had fielded such outstanding teams. When the team left Brooklyn, the alleged culprit was the Dodgers' owner, Walter O'Malley, who was a part owner of Brooklyn Union Gas and the

(Above) Ticket to opening day at Ebbets Field. 1941. Brooklyn Historical Society.

Long Island Railroad. No name is more anathema to old Brooklynites than that of O'Malley.

In 1958, the team became the Los Angeles Dodgers. In sunny southern California, Sandy Koufax, the pride of Bensonhurst, established himself as one of the most dominant pitchers in baseball history.

Professional baseball returned to Brooklyn, however, in the summer of 2001, when the Cyclones began playing at a brand-new ballpark in Coney Island. KeySpan Park, seating 7,500 spectators, stands on land once part of the famous Steeplechase Park, whose closing in 1964 was a blow to Brooklyn's identity almost as serious as the Dodgers' move to the West Coast.

The Cyclones, whose name derives from Coney's legendary roller coaster a few blocks from the stadium, are a Class A farm team belonging to the New York Mets. (The National League established the Mets in Queens in 1962, in part to placate sad Brooklynites. While the Mets are considered "Brooklyn's team," many Brooklynites prefer to root against the Yankees rather than to root for the Mets.) Old-timers as well as a new generation of baseball enthusiasts revel in watching pro ball in Brooklyn. The Cyclones, without question, add to Brooklyn's reputation as a baseball city.

An old Brooklyn baseball tradition is the way in which Brooklyn boys (and sometimes girls) adapted the game to the narrow confines of the borough's tenement and rowhouse streets. "Stickball" employs a sticklike bat (sometimes a broom handle) and a rubber ball (often called a "spaldeen," after the rubber-ball manufacturer Spalding). Basic baseball rules apply, with streetside adaptations, often varying from neighborhood to neighborhood. If the ball hits a roof or breaks a window, it's an automatic out. (Such events usually also mean that the game is over.) Stickballers measure a hitter's prowess by how far a ball is hit, with distances rendered by number of manhole covers. Young Brooklynites could dream of being the Duke of Flatbush.

(Above) Alexandra Stonehill. Ticket window at KeySpan Park. 2003.

STAGE STRUCK

BROOKLYN'S MOVIE PALACES

No movie theater was more dazzling than the Brooklyn Paramount. Still standing today at the corner of Flatbush and DeKalb, the Paramount opened in 1928, during the brief period when movie theaters were palatial and opulent in design. Such theaters provided an escape from reality, sometimes surpassing even the movies shown on the screen.

The Brooklyn Paramount was an example of what the architectural press of the time called an "atmospheric theater . . . in which the scenic effects are not confined to the stage." Seating an audience

of over 4,000, the Paramount had a richly gilded ceiling, elaborate fountains, and "color organs" that sprayed light through colored filters across the theater. Designed by noted theater architects

Rapp & Rapp of Chicago, the Paramount was one of the most spectacular of the hundreds of movie palaces created by that firm.

"These are part of a celestial city," George Rapp wrote, in describing his theaters, "whose iridescent lights and luxurious fittings heighten expectation of pleasure. It is richness unabashed, but richness with a reason." The reason was simple: to attract moviegoers to the box office.

Between 1928 and 1962, the Paramount presented not only motion pictures, but stage shows. Legend has it that George Gershwin first met Ethel Merman at the Brooklyn Paramount, and that Ginger Rogers danced there before she met Fred Astaire. In 1931, crooner Russ Columbo set a Paramount attendance record that stood until 1955, when a WINS disc jockey named Alan

(Above) Brooklyn Paramount handbill. 1955. Private collection. (Opposite) Brooklyn Paramount Theater. 1948. Collection Brian Merlis.

Freed presented his legendary rock-and-roll stage shows. Some say that Freed actually coined the term "rock and roll." A typical early show, in April 1955, featured La Vern Baker, the Penguins, Eddie Fontaine, the Chuckles, and Red Prysock. These shows helped to make the new music so wildly popular that Brooklyn became the center of live rock-and-roll. The teen-aged audiences—often waiting in long lines to get into the theater—sang along and danced in the aisles. Freed's competitor as a rock impresario was Murray the K, and both he and Freed staged programs at the Paramount and, down the street, at the Fox.

The Paramount closed in August, 1962, with a showing of the Howard Hawks film *Hatari*. The space now functions as the Athletic Center of Long Island University. Much of its original décor is intact, as is the famous Wurlitzer organ, now played to whip up the crowd at basketball games of the LIU Blackbirds.

Brooklyn's second largest theater, the Loew's Kings in Flatbush, is a 1929 gem decorated in a spectacular French Baroque style, with a massive dome, an ornate terra-cotta façade, and seating for 3,600. Designed by Rapp & Rapp, the theater is a sad reminder of the golden days of movie palaces. Loew's Kings closed in 1977. While the theater awaited demolition, Brooklynites persuaded the city to buy the Kings. Locked and derelict, it now awaits restoration. Many remember the Loew's Kings as the theater where Barbra Streisand worked as an usher when she was a student at Erasmus Hall High School.

Downtown Brooklyn was a movie theater mecca in the first half of the twentieth century. The RKO Albee, built in the 1920s, stood on Fleet Street, where a shopping mall now stands. The Fox (1928) was on Flatbush and Livingston, on the site of the Verizon Building. The Strand (1919) and the Majestic (1903) stood side by side on Fulton and Rockwell Place. Both of these still stand, though the Strand is now home to a Brooklyn institution of more recent vintage, Urban Glass, a studio for fine glass art. In the 1980s, the Brooklyn Academy of Music imaginatively restored the long-abandoned Majestic, now the Harvey Theater.

Brooklyn's most important performing arts institution is undoubtedly the Brooklyn Academy of Music, affectionately known as BAM. When its first building opened in 1861, BAM was part of a great cultural nucleus on or near Montague Street in Brooklyn Heights. Its neighbors included the Brooklyn Art Association and the Mercantile Library, important institutions that predate the Brooklyn Museum and the Brooklyn Public Library. Around the corner, on Pierrepont Street, the Long Island Historical Society—now the Brooklyn Historical Society—opened in 1881 in what many consider

THE BROOKLYN ACADEMY OF MUSIC.—INTERIOR. OPENING CONCERT ON TUESDAY, JANUARY 15, 1861.—[See Page 78.]

one of the city's architectural treasures. This newly restored building is a vital resource for anyone interested in Brooklyn history.

BAM assumed a national reputation during these early years, hosting famous performers from around the world. Edwin Booth, Ellen Terry, John Drew, and Eleonora Duse all graced BAM's stage on Montague Street. When the building burned down in 1903, its directors made the bold decision to erect a new, improved Brooklyn Academy of Music on Lafayette Avenue, in the Fort Greene neighborhood. Henry Herts and Hugh Tallant designed the new BAM, which opened in 1908.

Opening night featured the legendary Enrico Caruso and Geraldine Farrar in Gounod's *Faust*, commencing the Metropolitan Opera Company's thirteen-year run at BAM. In 1920, on BAM's stage, during the Met's production of Donizetti's *L'Elisir d'amore*, Caruso suffered the throat hemorrhage that ended his career. Coughing up blood while singing, he continued with his performance until the end of the first act. The 3,000 opera lovers attending the performance sat

(Above) *The Brooklyn Academy of Music opening concert.* **January 15, 1861. The New York Public Library.**

stunned as the curtain failed to rise for Act II. Caruso died a few months later.

In spite of BAM's illustrious history, the economic decline of downtown Brooklyn in the post–World War II years took its toll on the great institution. There was even talk of turning the elegant opera house into tennis courts. But in 1967, an enterprising Brooklyn native named Harvey Lichtenstein took over as BAM's president and executive producer. Under his leadership, BAM entered upon a new phase of glory. With its Next Wave festival, inaugurated in 1981, BAM became America's leading venue for the avant-garde, featuring premieres of works by Peter Brook, Philip Glass, Steve Reich, William Bolcom, John Adams, Ingmar Bergman, Robert Wilson, Laurie Anderson,

Merce Cunningham, Twyla Tharp, Mark Morris, and Pina Bausch, among others.

BAM's move into a second building in the neighborhood, in 1987—restoring the old Majestic and renaming it the Harvey, after Harvey Lichtenstein—sparked the ambitious idea of creating a cultural district in the area. The Mark Morris Dance Center is already in operation. Studios and rehearsal spaces for local arts groups are now in the works. The latest proposal is an innovative new Brooklyn Library for the Visual and Performing Arts, to be built just across Ashland Place from BAM's main building.

From the period of its explosive growth in the mid-nineteenth century, Brooklyn was an important center of the performing arts

(Above) The Brooklyn Academy of Music vintage postcard. 1913. Private collection.

in America. Today's renaissance of performance in Brooklyn mirrors the glories of the past.

MOVIE-MAKING IN BROOKLYN

Vitagraph, one of the major production companies in the early history of American movies, built its first studio in Brooklyn in 1905, in Midwood. Although this was a time when movie companies made one-reel silent films, each ten to fifteen minutes long, Vitagraph boldly decided that the future was in longer feature films. By 1912, this innovative studio produced a three-reel movie each week, using their stock company of 400 actors. Some say that Leon Trotsky worked as an extra on several Vitagraph movies made in Brooklyn, earning $5 a day.

One of the greatest pioneers in filmmaking was the co-founder of Vitagraph, J. Stuart Blackton, considered "equal in artistic

importance to D. W. Griffith." In 1907, Blackton's *Haunted Hotel* was the first film in which a filmmaker animated real, not drawn, objects through frame-by-frame photography, a technique known in this country as "pixilation," but known in France as *mouvement americain*.

Vitagraph's biggest star was Norma Talmadge, who grew up in Brooklyn, attended Erasmus Hall High School, and began working at the studio when she was still a teenager. Although she is little known today, she was a superstar of the silent cinema—one of the top box-office draws in the early 1920s. Talmadge left Vitagraph to form her own film company, but her career ended when "talking pictures" became popular in the late 1920s.

In its heyday, Vitagraph's five studios extended over two blocks in Midwood, with another studio in Long Island's Bay Shore, offices in London and Paris, and a studio in Los Angeles.

(Above) Alexandra Stonehill. Photograph of BAM's Harvey Theater. 2003.

The company set up a facility in California in 1911 and within a few years most of its production took place out there. In 1925, Warner Brothers bought Vitagraph.

Eventually, new owners divided the Vitagraph site at East 15th Street and Avenue M into two parcels, with a yeshiva next to NBC's broadcast studios. Over the years, NBC taped many television shows here, including the early color "Spectaculars," the soap opera "Another World," and the hit series "The Cosby Show." If any ghosts from the Vitagraph days should come back to roam about these buildings, they would feel at home on the stages of this historic site.

FIRST NATIONAL FILM

Brooklyn (and Brooklynites) starred in many movies. Gene Kelly danced over the Brooklyn Bridge in *On the Town* (1949), Coney Island was the setting for the first Keystone Comedies (1912), Bay

Ridge starred in *Saturday Night Fever* (1978), and F. Scott Fitzgerald even wrote a script entitled *Brooklyn Bridge* (1940, but never produced).

Since the mid-1980s, Spike Lee has used Brooklyn as a stage set. One of the most important filmmakers of his generation, Lee made his first movie—*Joe's Bed-Stuy Barbershop: We Cut Heads*—while he was a graduate student in New York University's film program. He went on to shoot *She's Gotta Have It* in Fort Greene (1986), *Do the Right Thing* in Bedford-Stuyvesant (1989), *Jungle Fever* in Bensonhurst (1991), and *He Got Game* in Coney Island (1998). As a writer, director, and producer, Spike Lee has created several dozen films about social issues. His production company, Forty Acres and a Mule (named after an order given by General William Tecumseh Sherman to provide land and an army mule to all displaced blacks after the Civil War), is located in Fort Greene.

(Above) Norma Talmadge vintage postcard. c. 1920. Private collection. (Opposite) Vitagraph handbill. c. 1917. Collection Brian Merlis.

HOMETOWN OF THE STARS (Born, Bred, or Based in Brooklyn): Bud Abbott • F. Murray Abraham • Woody Allen • Lauren Bacall • Eubie Blake • Joe Bolognav • Clara Bow • Mel Brooks • Lenny Bruce • Eddie Cantor • Betty Carter • Harry Chapin • Betty Comden • Aaron Copland • Vic Damone • Marion Davies • Dom DeLuise • Neil Diamond • Harvey Fierstein • Fyvush Finkel • Vincent Gardenia • George Gershwin • Jackie Gleason • Lou Gossett, Jr. • Elliott Gould • Arlo Guthrie • Buddy Hackett • Moss Hart • Susan Hayward • Rita Hayworth • Gregory Hines • Lena Horne • Edward Everett Horton •

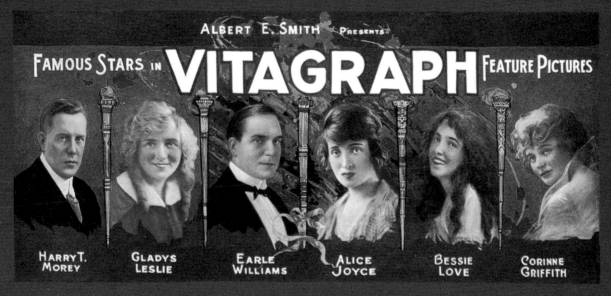

Harry Houdini • Emil Jannings • Danny Kaye • Harvey Keitel • Alan King • Carole King • Larry King • Veronica Lake • Spike Lee • Barry Manilow • Anne Meara • Robert Merrill • Mary Tyler Moore • Cousin Brucie Morrow • Zero Mostel • Joseph Papp • Buddy Rich • The Ritz Brothers • Joan Rivers • Chris Rock • Mickey Rooney • Neil Sedaka • Beverly Sills • Phil Silvers • Neil Simon • Paul Sorvino • Barbara Stanwyck • Barbara Streisand • Joan Sutherland • Irving Thalberg • Marisa Tomei • Richard Tucker • John Turturro • Brenda Vaccaro • Ben Vereen • Eli Wallach • Mae West • Shelley Winters • Henny Youngman •

TO·THE·DEFENDERS·OF·THE·UNION 1861 1865

CULTURAL ODYSSEY:
ART * BOOKS * COLLECTIONS

WILLIAM MERRITT CHASE

For a time, Brooklyn harbored the painter William Merritt Chase, one of the most admired artists of America's Gilded Age. Born in Indiana in 1849, Chase came to New York to study at the National Academy of Design. He later went to the Royal Academy in Munich, where he developed a style heavily influenced by the Spanish master Diego Velázquez. In 1878, Chase returned to New York and became one of the era's most important teachers of painting. (His students included Georgia O'Keeffe, George Bellows, Rockwell Kent, and Charles Sheeler.) He taught for several years at the Brooklyn Art Association.

Chase lived as an aesthete in New York City, in settings both opulent and bohemian. But he also lived and worked more quietly in a genteel, bourgeois neighborhood called Bedford-Stuyvesant in Brooklyn. Residing in his father's house on Marcy Avenue, near Tompkins Park, Chase sought his subject in the Brooklyn scene. His plein air pictures of Prospect Park, Tompkins Park, Bath Beach, Gowanus Bay, the Navy Yard, and his own Bedford-Stuyvesant backyard captured the borough of homes and churches, parks and beaches as did no other visual artist of that time.

The lush greenery, sun-dappled water, strolling women in their Victorian finery, and

(Above) J. Carroll Beckwith. *Portrait of William Merritt Chase*. 1881–82. Indianapolis Museum of Art.
(Opposite) The Soldiers' and Sailors' Memorial Arch, Grand Army Plaza vintage postcard. c. 1900. Private collection.

stately churches that we see in Chase's paintings remind us of a long-ago Brooklyn, different from the iconic borough of stevedoring, stickball playing, trolley-dodging, and roller-coaster riding. Chase's Brooklyn scenes remind us as does nothing else of the infinite horizon of Brooklyn life. Take away either the clipped hedges of genteel squares or the noisome roar of waterfront factories, either the proper cadences of New England–descended speech or the loquacious thunder of Bensonhurst Brooklynese, and you sever something vital from Brooklyn, a place of joyous contradictions.

THE BROOKLYN MUSEUM OF ART

The majestic Brooklyn Museum of Art, one of the world's great museums, stands on the northern end of Institute Park, adjacent to the Brooklyn Botanic Garden. Brooklyn civic leaders began planning the museum before the Consolidation of the boroughs of New York took place in 1898, but did not make much of a start on it until Brooklyn became part of New York City. After Consolidation, Brooklyn scaled back many of its projects, including the museum.

Vast and splendid as the Brooklyn Museum of Art is today, its founders intended it to be nearly four times larger. Only the central portion and one wing of the Beaux-Arts building were completed. Designed by McKim, Mead & White (chosen in an architectural competition), the building rose in phases between the 1890s and 1915. The museum lost its monumental exterior stairway in a 1930s remodeling, which also produced the present austere lobby. In 2004, the museum completed a major expansion by adding a pavilion and public plaza at the museum's entrance. Designed by Polshek Partnership Architects,

(Above) Georgia O'Keeffe. Brooklyn Bridge. 1948. Brooklyn Museum of Art.

the new space is a daring twenty-first-century addition to a nine-teenth-century landmark.

The permanent collection of this renowned museum includes more than a million-and-a-half objects, ranging from ancient art to contemporary photographs. The world-famous Egyptian collection alone makes a visit to the museum worthwhile. Other highlights include its Asian art, its large holdings of African art (the Brooklyn Museum was the first in America to display African objects as art), and its collection of American paintings. A pioneer in the installation of period rooms, the museum includes an entire seventeenth-century Dutch farmhouse from Flatlands. The museum's curators continually present interesting and often-provocative temporary exhibitions that draw large audiences.

The newly restored granite sculptures flanking the museum's entrance originally stood on pylons at the Brooklyn approach to the Manhattan Bridge. When the city widened the roadway in the 1960s, the sculptures moved there. Created by Daniel Chester French, the allegorical groups represent the two boroughs. The female figure of Manhattan is imperious, proud, and rich (her right foot rests upon a treasure chest). Brooklyn, in contrast, represents nobler virtues. A civic crown adorns her head. To her right are a tree and a child reading a book, while to her left are a church and emblems of art.

Looking at the museum from Eastern Parkway, one sees a series of thirty statues at the building's attic level. This diverse group represents important figures from the world's cultures, from Confucius to Mohammed to Julius Caesar. In the back of the museum, in the Frieda Schiff Warburg Sculpture Garden, one finds architectural ornaments salvaged from demolished buildings from all five boroughs (including a lion's head from Steeplechase Park).

(Above) Brooklyn Museum of Art from Eastern Parkway. Vintage postcard. c. 1940. Private collection.

PUBLIC SCULPTURE

Public sculpture graces streets and squares, parks and gardens, and building façades throughout Brooklyn. Its memorials, monuments, fountains, and statues rank with the best of any American city.

Such works include Henry Merwin Shrady's superb equestrian statue of George Washington, in the shadow of the Williamsburg Bridge (1901–06); John Quincy Adams Ward's statue of Henry Ward Beecher, in Cadman Plaza (1891); William Ordway Partridge's equestrian statue of Ulysses S. Grant, in front of the Union League Club at Grant Square (1896); and many others.

The greatest of Brooklyn's works of public art adorn Grand Army Plaza, where Prospect Park West, Flatbush Avenue, and Eastern Parkway meet in a storm of traffic. The spectacular triumphal arch, the Soldiers' and Sailors' Monument, memorializes the Union forces that died in the Civil War. Designed by John H. Duncan, the granite arch provides the perfect setting for sculpture. Architect Stanford White oversaw the arch's sculpture, giving the commission to a native Brooklynite, Frederick W. MacMonnies, one of the greatest of American sculptors.

Atop the arch is Columbia Triumphant, raising her wreathed scepter, in a chariot pulled by four horses. On the piers facing Prospect Park are two groups by MacMonnies. On the left is Army, an amazingly intricate scene brimming with violent action, a vision in bronze of Stephen Crane's Red Badge of Courage. The commander in the foreground, his sword raised high, is a self-portrait of sculptor MacMonnies. On the opposite pier is the Navy, depicting sailors awaiting their fate on the deck of a sinking ship.

Sculpture abounds in Grand Army Plaza. Of special note, just inside Prospect Park, is a superb statue of James Stranahan by MacMonnies, his earliest public commission. Without Stranahan, Prospect Park might not exist. He recognized and encouraged Calvert Vaux's genius. It is fitting that Marianne Moore enjoined all who entered Prospect Park to tip their hats to Mr. Stranahan.

THE ART SCENE

Brooklyn writers far outnumbered artists until a few years ago, when an astonishing number of painters, sculptors, filmmakers, and photographers crossed the river and settled here. They created high-ceilinged, light-flooded studios and homes in abandoned nineteenth-century warehouses and industrial buildings. Their neighborhoods were soon chock-a-block with galleries, cafes, bookstores, and nightspots.

The new artists' colonies include Williamsburg and DUMBO (an acronym for "Down Under the Manhattan Bridge Overpass"), each only one subway stop from Manhattan. At this writing, Williamsburg boasts nearly forty galleries, mainly in its Northside neighborhood. Its lively art scene is reviewed by international critics and followed closely by collectors of the avant-garde. The smallest art space, Holland Tunnel, is a gallery in a garden shed. A few blocks away, a larger exhibition of art is shown on three floors of an 1868 Victorian bank building, now the Williamsburg Art and Historical Center.

The fifteen-square blocks of DUMBO resound with creative energy. Artists have converted Civil War–era coffee and tea warehouses to workshops and studios, many of which are open to visitors during the annual arts festival. On Water Street, St. Ann's Warehouse has created an innovative off-off Broadway theater in an old spice factory. Summer exhibitions and performances take place in the interior of the Brooklyn Bridge Anchorage. Nearby, for more than a quarter of a century, Bargemusic has presented nationally renowned chamber music performances in its floating concert hall at the foot of Old Fulton Street.

BOOKS

The Brooklyn Public Library, facing onto Grand Army Plaza, is the main branch of one of America's largest public library systems. Designed in a striking Art Moderne style by the archi-

(Above) Brooklyn trade card. John Baldwin's Sons, Tea, Coffee, Wine and Liquor Merchants, Grand Street, Brooklyn trade card. c. 1870. Private collection.

tects Alfred Githens and Francis Keally, the library opened in 1941 to rave reviews by many architectural critics. Carl Paul Jennewein designed the gilded reliefs on the curving piers at the entrance, while Thomas H. Jones created the bronze screen. Drawn from literature, the figures on the screen include Washington Irving's Rip Van Winkle, Herman Melville's Moby Dick, and the image of Brooklyn's own Walt Whitman.

Inside is the dramatic, three-story-high catalogue room, one of Brooklyn's

most impressive interior spaces. Upstairs, the library's Brooklyn Collection is a priceless resource for anyone interested in the history of the city and borough of Brooklyn. Books, atlases, maps, memorabilia, and more than 35,000 photographs provide information to researchers, filmmakers, genealogists, and students.

The collection also includes the newspaper clipping files of the Brooklyn *Daily Eagle*, as well as a complete run of this newspaper (1841–1955) on microfilm.

In addition to the central library, the system comprises a vast network of nearly sixty neighborhood branch libraries, most of them created under the Carnegie bequest. The popular Kidsmobile, a children's library-on-wheels, visits many Brooklyn neighborhoods. That Brooklyn has its own independent library system, separate from that of New York, reminds us that, though no longer a separate city, Brooklyn retains an independent spirit.

🐢 🐢 🐢 🐢 🐢

During the nineteenth century, several private subscription libraries flourished in Brooklyn. The Apprentices' Library (founded

A BROOKLYN STREETSCAPE

(Lower right) E. H. Wallop for New York Road Runners. 2002. New York City Marathon runners in Brooklyn streets.
(All other photographs) Alexandra Stonehill. 2003. Smith Street restaurant, Fort Greene cafe, and Park Slope rowhouses.

in 1823) and the Mercantile Library (1857) charged an annual fee for their use. Walt Whitman, in *Specimen Days*, recalls working as a young boy for a lawyer who gave him a subscription to a Brooklyn circulating library. "I now revel'd in romance-reading of all kinds; first, the 'Arabian Nights,' all the volumes . . . then, Walter Scott's novels, one after another, and his poetry." Not until 1896 did the philanthropist Charles Pratt open the Free Library, the first that permitted all Brooklyn residents over the age of fourteen to borrow books without paying a fee.

Brooklyn welcomed two publishing houses that moved from New York to Williamsburg in the 1860s. The D. Appleton Company opened a printing and bookbinding plant with 600 workers. Known for publishing religious books, travel books, textbooks, and science books (including Darwin's *The Origin of Species*), Appleton's printed 1,000 books a day during its peak years. McLoughlin Brothers, a children's book publisher, printed popular classics and board games. Eventually, the Milton Bradley Toy Company bought McLoughlin's.

While many cities bemoan that they have fewer bookstores than in the past, in Brooklyn today bookstores flourish as never before. This is unsurprising given the large numbers of writers and editors who call Brooklyn home. In Park Slope, famously a writers' neighborhood, no fewer than six bookstores are located along one eleven-block stretch of Seventh Avenue. Williamsburg, Brooklyn Heights, Cobble Hill, and other Brooklyn neighborhoods boast excellent bookstores, from secondhand to national chains to several of New York City's finest independent booksellers.

COLLECTIONS

The most comprehensive collection of Brooklyn-related materials is at the Brooklyn Historical Society, one of the oldest and most important institutions of its kind in the country. Founded in 1863, the Society (originally known as the Long Island Historical Society) moved into its present building, on Pierrepont and Clinton Streets, in 1881. Designed by George B. Post, the building is one of Brooklyn's architectural gems, particularly now, after the recent

(Opposite) *Grand Opening March Over the Brooklyn Bridge*. **Punch cartoon. 1883. The Brooklyn Historical Society.**

renovation that cleaned and repointed the unique brick and terra-cotta façade.

One of the Brooklyn Historical Society's glories is its library, among the finest historical repositories in the city, with more than 155,000 volumes. This collection includes genealogies, rare books, newspapers, personal papers, journals, and oral histories that document Brooklyn's many ethnic groups and neighborhoods. Highlights include a copy of the Emancipation Proclamation signed by Abraham Lincoln, the papers of Henry Ward Beecher, and the Pierrepont papers dealing with slavery and abolition. Researchers also prize the Society for its collection of more than 33,000 photographs, drawings, and paintings of Brooklyn landmarks, streets, neighborhoods, and residents. In addition to exhibitions on Brooklyn history, the Society offers educational programs including walking tours of Brooklyn history and architecture.

Opening in 1899, The Brooklyn Children's Museum pioneered the interactive, hands-on exhibits now standard in museums. In its early days, the museum collections included natural history specimens such as birds, insects, shells, and minerals. Today, the museum has a wide-ranging collection of more than 27,000 objects. A favorite of many children is the Portable Collection Program, in which the young people borrow objects to take home to study them up-close.

In 1977, the museum moved out of the pair of old Crown Heights mansions that had been its home for many years, into a

(Above) Alexandra Stonehill. Brooklyn Historical Society facade (detail), 2003.

new building designed by Hardy Holzman Pfeiffer Associates, on the corner of St. Mark's and Brooklyn Avenues. At the time, *The New York Times* described the museum as "a sort of learned funhouse—a collection of educational exhibitions housed in a wildly exuberant structure that is itself the best exhibition of all." The Children's Museum plans an expansion, designed by Rafael Viñoly, with a two-story addition encompassed by a bold yellow façade.

Housed in a 1936 subway station (now decommissioned), the New York Transit Museum explores the history of mass transit. Urban historians, subway buffs, and curious kids flock to this fascinating museum, located in downtown Brooklyn at the corner of Boerum Place and Schermerhorn Street.

The museum's idiosyncratic collection includes vintage subway cars dating back to 1904, old wooden turnstiles, an exhibit of station mosaics, hundreds of subway signs, architectural drawings of ticket booths, and a display of more than 200 trolley models. A recent major renovation added children's classrooms, a resource center, and a reference library to the museum. Occasionally, the Transit Museum organizes a trip on the Nostalgia Train, taking passengers on vintage 1927 D-type Triplex cars on a ride that wends through Brooklyn to Coney Island.

(Above) Byron Studio. Trolleys bound for Prospect Park. 1899. New York Bound Archives.

MANHATTAN

Green-
point

Williams-
burg

QUEENS

Fort
Greene

Bushwick

Brooklyn Heights

Bedford Stuyvesant

Red
Hook

Crown
Heights

East
New York

Park
Slope

Prospect
Lefferts
Gardens

PROSPECT
PARK

Prospect

Brownsville

GREEN-WOOD
CEMETERY

Sunset Park

Flatbush

Borough Park

Canarsie

Flatlands

Bay
Ridge

Bensonhurst

Midwood

Gravesend

Sheepshead Bay

Brighton
Beach

Coney Island

"There seems almost no
conceivable end to Brooklyn ...
horizon beyond horizon forever
unfolded, an immeasurable
proliferation of house on house
and street by street"

— JAMES AGEE

Map by Susan DeVries

A GASTRONOMIC ADVENTURE

Walking through the streets of Brooklyn can be an architectural exercise or a cultural expedition or a gastronomic adventure. Brooklyn's diverse, vibrant neighborhoods are inhabited by more than 150 nationalities, each celebrating its own culinary heritage.

Brighton Beach serves caviar blini and Ukrainian borscht in its boardwalk cafes, thanks to the recent Russian émigrés. Atlantic Avenue's grocery stores burgeon with shelves of Middle Eastern spices and jars of rosepetal jam. Crown Heights's specialties include West Indian coconut bread and curried goat. Greenpoint, often called Little Poland, features kielbasa and pierogis, and perhaps more pork per square block than any neighborhood in America. Bay Ridge's seafaring Scandinavian population has dwindled, but you can still find smoked fish and Swedish limpa bread there. In Bensonhurst, the largest Italian neighborhood in New York, the salumerias sell homemade pasta and more than 30 kinds of cheese.

Restaurants are booming in Brooklyn, from the venerable nineteenth century Peter Luger in Williamsburg and Gage & Tollner in downtown Brooklyn, to the trendy new bistros on Smith Street, DeKalb Avenue, Columbia Street, and Fifth Avenue. If you're still hungry, go to Junior's on Flatbush Avenue, which bakes a thousand cheesecakes every day, or to the Brooklyn Ice Cream Factory, whipping up batches of ice cream in a former firehouse at the Fulton Ferry Landing, or to its neighbor on Water Street, Jacques Torres Chocolate, already a legend to anyone with a sweet tooth. And don't forget that Brooklyn boasts the best pizza and the best beer in the metropolitan region.

The foods of Brooklyn—whether purchased in restaurants or grocery stores, or from take-out shops or curbside vendors—remind us of the homelands of those whose arduous voyages brought them from afar to realize their dreams in Brooklyn.

LIST OF
ILLUSTRATIONS

Page 50 (right). Arthur Leipzig. *Brooklyn Bridge*. 1946. Photograph courtesy of Howard Greenberg Gallery, New York.

Page 51. Verrazano–Narrows Bridge. 1965. Photograph from MTA Bridges and Tunnels Special Archive.

Page 52. Brooklyn Approach to the Williamsburg Bridge vintage postcard. 1905. Private collection.

Page 53. Brooklyn Bridge from the Brooklyn side. 1903. Photograph by the Detroit Publishing Company. New York Bound Archives.

Page 54. William Merritt Chase. *The Church of the Puritans*. 1887. Oil on panel. Collection of George H. Meyer.

Page 57. Testimony in the Great Beecher-Tilton Scandal. c. 1875. Library of Congress.

Page 58. Beecher Statue in Downtown Brooklyn. c. 1910. Photograph from New York Bound Archives.

Pages 60–61. Notorious Navy Yard Gang after confessing to murder of Brooklyn druggist. February 27, 1922. Photograph from Bettmann/Corbis.

Page 62. Gangsters linked to Brooklyn. May 2, 1933. Photograph from Bettmann/Corbis.

Page 63. Alexandra Stonehill. Photograph of Montauk Club (detail), Brooklyn. 2003.

Page 64. Ebbets Field vintage postcard. 1943. Private collection.

Page 65. Brooklyn baseball team. 1899. Photograph from New York Bound Archives.

Page 67. Leo Durocher at a Brooklyn Dodgers baseball game. 1942. Photograph from Hulton-Deutsch Collection/Corbis.

(Above) Brooklyn Marathon. February 12, 1909. Library of Congress.

Page 68. William Klein. *"Let's Go Dodgers."* Dodgers fans at Ebbets Field. 1955. Photograph courtesy of Howard Greenberg Gallery, New York.

Page 69. Jackie Robinson scoring a home-run. August 4, 1948. Photograph from New York Bound Archives.

Page 70. Ticket to opening day at Ebbets Field. 1941. Brooklyn Historical Society.

Page 71. Alexandra Stonehill. Photograph of ticket window at KeySpan Park. 2003.

Page 72. Brooklyn Paramount Theater. 1941. Photograph from Collection of Brian Merlis.

Page 73. Brooklyn Paramount handbill. 1955. Private collection.

Page 75. *The Brooklyn Academy of Music opening concert*. January 15, 1861. Picture Collection, The Branch Libraries. The New York Public Library, Astor, Lenox and Tilden Foundations.

Page 76. The Brooklyn Academy of Music vintage postcard. 1913. Private collection.

Page 77. Alexandra Stonehill. Photograph of BAM's Harvey Theater. 2003.

Pages 78. Norma Talmadge vintage post-card. c. 1920. Private collection.

Page 79. Vitagraph handbill. c. 1917. Collection of Brian Merlis.

Page 80. The Soldiers' and Sailors' Memorial Arch, Grand Army Plaza vintage postcard. c. 1900. Private collection.

Page 81. J. Carroll Beckwith. *Portrait of William Merritt Chase*. 1881–82. Oil on canvas. Indianapolis Museum of Art, Gift of the Artist.

Page 82. Georgia O'Keeffe. *Brooklyn Bridge*. 1948. Oil on masonite. Brooklyn Museum of Art. Bequest of Mary Childs Draper. Artists Rights Society (ARS), New York.

Page 83. Brooklyn Museum of Art from Eastern Parkway vintage postcard. c. 1940. Private collection.

Page 85. Trade card for John Baldwin's Sons, Tea, Coffee, Wine and Liquor Merchants, Grand Street, Brooklyn. c. 1870. Private collection.

Page 86. Alexandra Stonehill. Photograph of Brooklyn Public Library entrance. 2003.

Page 87. (lower right) E. H. Wallop for New York Road Runners. New York City Marathon runners in Brooklyn. 2002. (all other photographs) Alexandra Stonehill. Photographs of Fort Greene café, Brooklyn Heights carriage house, Park Slope brown-stones, and Smith Street restaurant. 2003.

Page 89. *Grand Opening March Over the Brooklyn Bridge*. 1883. Punch cartoon. The Brooklyn Historical Society.

Page 90. Alexandra Stonehill. Photograph of Brooklyn Historical Society (detail). 2003.

Page 91. Byron Studio. Trolleys bound for Prospect Park. 1899. Photograph from New York Bound Archives.

Page 92. Map designed by Susan DeVries. 2003.

Page 95. Brooklyn Marathon. February 12, 1909. Photograph from the Library of Congress.

Page 96. Trade card for Cable Screw Wire, showing East River Suspension Bridge. c. 1875. Chromolithograph. Collection of The New-York Historical Society.

200 Tons of Cable Screw Wire used in 1874 in making Boots & Shoes.

TRY OUR

CABLE SCREW WIRE BOOTS & SHOES.

THE True Way TO MAKE A Shoe or Bridge.

THE EAST RIVER BRIDGE BETWEEN BROOKLYN & NEW YORK.

(Above) Cable Screw Wire trade card, showing East River Suspension Bridge. c. 1875. The New-York Historical Society.